Information Technology and Library Automation

Information Technology and Library Automation

G. Devarajan
Ravindran Asari K

Ess Ess Publications
New Delhi

Information Technology and Library Automation

ISBN: 978-81-7000-723-4

₹ 500/-

First Published 2014

Published by:
Ess Ess Publications
4831/24, Ansari Road,
Darya Ganj,
New Delhi-110 002.
INDIA
Phones: 23260807, 41563444
Fax: 41563334
E-mail: info@essessreference.com
www.essessreference.com

Cover Design by *Patch Creative Unit*

Printed and bound in India at Salasar Imaging Systems.

Contents

PREFACE

Information is an international resource and valuable input for societal development. The information revolution makes development speedier than ever before. Now the avenues in new information technologies and plummeting computing costs are sticking distance and eroding borders and time. Today the remotest village has the possibility of tapping a global source of information which was beyond the dreams of anyone living decades ago.

Technological change is a major contributor to economic development. The rapid development of information and information technology has tremendously increased our capacity to process information and accelerated growth in the information intensive sector. The impact of information technology arises from its attributes such as enabling technology which can be applied in a wide range of different circumstances, the capacity of the technology increasing at an exponential rate; and the cost of the technology falling rapidly. These attributes of information technology will trigger a new wave of economic growth stimulating the development of information society. It is indeed the avenues of information technology that should be utilised to the possible extent in libraries and information centres to make use of the information speedily, effectively, efficiently and with precision.

The main objective of this book is to give some idea to the library professionals about the information, communication technology and their applications in the library operations and services. The book is organised under seven chapters. The chapters are : Chapter 1—Information technology; Chapter 2 — Computer; Chapter 3 — Basic hardware; Chapter 4 — Software; Chapter 5 — Library automation; Chapter 6 — Library management software; and Chapter 7 — Computer networks. We strongly believe that the book will be highly useful to students in library and information science and practicing professionals engaged in information management.

Trivandrum **— Authors**

1

INFORMATION TECHNOLOGY

INTRODUCTION

Information Technology or IT in short, is the most dominant subject in the world today. It affects every sphere of human life. It has become an essential tool for doing almost all activities. It influences education, business and administration. It is now recognized that a natural place for its application in library, where traditionally information storage, processing and retrieval has been taking place. These traditional functions of the library can be made more easy and efficient with the application of IT.

Information has been the life blood of the human society ever since it emerged. As society grew information also got generated from time to time. One of the most important attributes of information is its exponential growth. It is estimated that the quantity of information in the world doubles every decade. Therefore, technologies available at any given time become insufficient to process, store and retrieve information. Therefore, newer techniques have been invented to make information more flexible and transparent. The milestone inventions in this direction are: the invention of paper, the invention of movable printing and the invention of digital technology. From the middle ages to the middle of the twentieth century, all knowledge of the global society had been preserved in the print media alone. But the exponential growth of information and information needs of the modern society have put new challenges to the print medium:

- It is difficult to choose a few relevant pieces of information from millions of pieces of information in the print medium.
- It has barriers of space and time.
- It needs more storage space.
- Cost of producing print on paper publications is on the increase.

The search for eliminating the above difficulties resulted in the development of a system for storing, processing and dissemination of information using machine. The binary language of '0' and '1' developed during the 1930s helped us to store and manipulate information using machine. Binary is another word for digital. The revolutionary changes brought about by the digital technology during the last eight decades can be comprehended by the term information technology (IT)

WHAT IS IT?

The invention of binary language (language using only two characters '0' and '1') opened the door for making information management more efficient. The first machine for storing binary data was created in 1945 – Electronic Numerical Integrator and Calculator (ENIAC) at the University of Pennsylvania in the US. We called it computer, because the dominant function of ENIAC was calculation (computing). The progress achieved by the computer field is astonishing. From ENIAC which weighed almost three tones and consumed 15000 watts of electricity to computers and computer devices that work on rechargeable button cells. Computers became smaller, grew in power as the prices came down.

The digital technology also revolutionized communication systems. In 1965 digital technology was used for transmitting information through communication channels. The use of digital technology in communication resulted in the development of long distance computer networks and transmission of digitized text and multimedia over computer networks. Now a computer without any network connectivity is not a fully functional computer.

All manuscripts were converted to printed form when movable printing technology was invented and new publications were brought out in print form only. This resulted in the establishment of publishing houses and libraries. Now with the invention of digital technology, printed books and journals are converted to digital media. With the commencement of digital or electronic publishing we have millions of digital/electronic books and thousands of e-journals, which are accessible through digital libraries and e-journal vendors. Now information can be accessed from remote servers through long distance computer networks from anywhere to anywhere without any time and geographical barrier.

When all these technologies – computer, communication and digital content – merged, a new multidisciplinary subject called information technology emerged. Information technology is defined as the combination of microelectronics based computer technology, communication technology and production, processing and dissemination of all forms of digitized information such as sound, text, graphics, animation and video. In fact, I.T is a combination of technologies such as computer technology, communication technology and digital technology.

IT has already become the symbol of development and it is influencing all spheres of human development. According to the Information Technology Association of America, "information technology can be defined as "the study, design, development, implementation, support or management of computer-based information systems, particularly software applications and computer hardware, data storage, database administration, and all other aspects related to information storage, retrieval, transmission, protection, and processing information". The term Information Technology was first used by **Leavitt and Whisler** in an article published in the Harvard Business Review in 1958 to describe a new technology that has started its revolution. Now the term has become the most popular and the techniques involved in IT controls every sphere of human life. Information Technology is now regarded as a tool to do all activities of the society in a better and more efficient manner. We have understood that IT is a composite subject and the components are mainly computer technology, communication technology and the digital technology that create, process and disseminate digital content. Let us examine each of these components in some detail.

COMPONENTS OF IT

1. Computer

It was in 1830s, a British mathematician first thought about the possibility of a computer. He was Charles Babbage – a professor of mathematics of the Cambridge University. He imagined the possibility of a mechanical device that would be able to store data and perform a number of calculations. Babbage was of the opinion that information could be manipulated by a machine if the information could be stored in the machine in the form of some codes. Babbage did use the terms as we use today to name the parts of the machine. The body of the machine he called 'mill' the memory was named 'store' and he thought of using some codes to store and process information. Anyway, he made a prototype of the modern computer model. That is why Charles Babbage is called the father of computer science.

Humanity had to wait another century for the real thing to happen. In the 1930s, Claude Shannon when he was a student demonstrated how a machine can store information and how it could follow logical instructions to manipulate information. A computer switch has two positions – an "on" position and "off" position. When it is on, it conveys the meaning 'true' and when it is off, it can convey the meaning 'false'. The on position could be represented by '1' and off position could be represented by '0'. This is the **binary system** – a language of only two characters. He put forward the idea that by logically combining 0s and 1s you can have a computer language. Binary system is the electronic language of the computer. It is also called **digital**.

Claude Shannon

A machine capable of storing binary information was developed in 1946. A group of mathematicians led by J. Presper Echert and John Mauchly developed a computer at the University of Pennsylvania's Moore School of Electrical Engineering on the principle developed by Shannon. The machine was called **Electronic Numerical Integrator and Calculator (ENIAC).** Thus the modern computer was born. It was a huge machine weighing 30 tons and occupied the entire space of a room measuring 30x50 feet. ENIAC consumed 150000 watts of energy and its memory was equivalent to just 80 characters. An ordinary calculator of today is at least 1000 times more powerful than ENIAC. Still it was a milestone, as digital storage of information was made possible. ENIAC was developed for performing calculations. That is why it got the name computer. Now computers do lesser calculations. They are now known for their capability for information storage, processing and retrieval.

The invention of transistor and integrated circuits made it possible to make the computers smaller and more powerful. The progress made during the last seven decades in the field of computer technology is astonishing. Drastic changes have taken place in the form, function, speed and size of computers and computer accessories like recording devices and printers. Now we have a variety of computers. Mainframes, mini computers, personal computers, lap tops, tablets, palm tops, etc. Computers are becoming smaller, growing in power as the prices are coming down. A modern computer is a machine that store, process and disseminate information.

Computer cannot work on its own. It needs specific instructions called programmes for carrying out each work. A computer is a general-purpose machine that processes data according to a set of instructions that are stored internally either temporarily or permanently. The computer and all equipment attached to it are called hardware. The instructions that tell the computer what to do are called **"software"**. A set of instructions that perform a particular task is called a "**programme**" or "**software programme**." Software packages are grouped under two major categories: **Application Software** and **System Software**. Software that has been developed to solve a particular problem, perform a useful work or provide entertainment is called **application software**. Software that controls the computer and enables the applications software to perform various activities is called **system software** or **operating systems.** Operating systems can perform without the help of application programs, but application programs cannot function without the help of operating systems. There another category of software called utility programmes. **Utility programmes** are used to perform activities like, setup a computer, format and partition disks and remove viruses. Utility programmes are regularly used by experts while ordinary users are more concerned with operating systems and application programmes. During the early period of computer development symbols were used to give instruction to a computer. They were called **symbolic languages** or **machine language.** After the mid 1970s words from the natural languages have been used for developing computer software. Therefore, developing computer software now-a-days involve natural language programming. More about computers will be included when discussing about types of computers and generations of computers.

"A computer is the most incredible tool we have ever seen"

— Steve Jobs

"A computer on every desk in every home running Microsoft Software" — **Bill gates**

2. Communication

Another area that form part of information technology is the developments in the communication field. Telecommunication is the electronic transfer of information from one location to another. The oldest and the largest communication network in the world is the telephone network. Graham Bell invented telephone in 1876. It was an analog system in which sound was converted into electrical vibrations and transmitted through wires. When telephone was invented, Graham Bell did not imagine that one day digital information could be transmitted through the telephone lines. Telecommunication system underwent drastic changes and at present its main function is transmission to digitized information and person to person interactive conversation has become a secondary job.

When telephone was started connection between two phones was achieved by what was called manual switching. In manual switching, when a person lift the telephone receiver, a light corresponding to that will glow in the telephone exchange. When a he/she dials a number, another light corresponding to that number will also glow in the exchange. An attendant in the telephone exchange manually connected these two telephones and conversation between two persons was made possible. It was called **manual switching**.

When telephone connections increased manual-connections became impossible. Then a mechanical device that worked with the help of electricity and magnetism was used to automatically connect between two lines. According to this system, when a number was dialed, automatically a lever was activated in the exchange and connection established between two lines. This method was called **electro-magnetic switching**. The system was an improvement compared to the manual switching, but it had to undergo frequent repairs as it was an analog system with moving parts and it sustained wear and tear.

Finally in 1965, when **digital switching** was invented, microprocessor based connections could be established between telephones and digital information could be transmitted through communication channels. There were no moving parts in the exchange and consequently no wear and tear. Digital switching made it possible to transmit not only sound but also all forms of digitized information. This paved the way for long distance computer networks or wide area networks.

COMMUNICATION MEDIA

Communication media are the physical channels through which information is transmitted between computers in a network. Media may be classified as bounded (i.e., wires, cables and optical fibbers) or unbounded (i.e., ether or airwaves through which radio, transmitted data can move along simplex, half-duplex or full- duplex lines depending on the needs and protocols involved.

BOUND MEDIA

Twisted - pair of wires are inexpensive media used in voice grade telephone lines. They are used for low speed transmission of signals of the order of 1200 bps. Coaxial cables can be used for high-speed data transmission over distance of several km. Coaxial cables have wide bandwidth of the order of 400 MHz. They may be used in LAN at transmission rates of about 1 Mega bps. Fiber Optics cables are glass fibres that provide high quality transmission of signals at very high speeds of nearly 1000 Megabits per second (Mbps) for distances up to 25 miles.

UNBOUND MEDIA

Radio wave in the very high frequency band (VHF) at about 300 MHz is used for communication between computers in inaccessible locations or for short-range communications. Microwaves are used for wide bandwidth line-of-sight communication. Rates of transmission up to 20 Giga bps are possible with this media. Communication satellite acts as microwave relay station is the sky. Transponders on the satellite are used to receive, amplify and retransmit signals sent from an earth station. The main advantage of satellite is its wide coverage of a large area and thus it may be used from inaccessible location. A transponder has a very large capacity and can handle about 400 channels, each channel having 64 kbps speed

COMMUNICATION CHANNELS

Also called a "circuit" or "line," it is a pathway over which data is transferred between remote devices. It may refer to the entire physical medium, such as a telephone line, optical fiber, coaxial cable or twisted wire pair, or, it may refer to one of several carrier frequencies transmitted simultaneously within the line. The word telephone was coined by combining tele and phonics (tele = long distance + phonics=sound). Thus telephone means long distance sound. Alexander Graham Bell's words, "Mr. Watson. Come here! I want you!" marked the beginning of the communication age.

TWISTED PAIR COPPER WIRE

The first commercial telephone service used twisted pair copper wire for providing telephone connectivity. Twisted pair is a thin-diameter wire (22 to 26 gauge) commonly used for telephone and network cabling. The wires are twisted around each other to minimize interference from other twisted pairs in the cable (Alexander Graham Bell invented this and was awarded a patent for it in 1881). Twisted pairs have less bandwidth than coaxial cable or optical fiber. Twisted pair cables are available unshielded (UTP) or shielded (STP). UTP is the most common. STP is used in noisy environments where the shield protects against excessive electromagnetic interference.

COAXIAL CABLE

A high-capacity cable used in communications and video, commonly called "co-ax." It contains an insulated solid or stranded wire surrounded by a solid or braided metallic shield, wrapped in a plastic cover. Fire-safe Teflon coating is optional. Although similar in appearance, there are several types of coaxial cables

OPTICAL FIBER

A thin glass strand designed for light transmission. A single hair-thin fiber is capable of transmitting millions of bits per second. In addition to their huge transmission capacity, optical fibers offer many advantages over copper wire. Data transmission is not affected by lightening and radiation. Compared to copper wire optical fiber is light weight.

WIRELESS COMMUNICATION MEDIA

Satellite

A radio relay station in orbit above the earth that receives, amplifies and redirects signals contained within a carrier frequency. There are hundreds of commercial communications satellites in orbit providing services for both industry and consumers. Wire free access to the Internet via satellite is becoming popular. Earth stations are required for transmitting/receiving signals in satellite communications. It uses a dish-shaped antenna for microwave transmission.

Microwave

Microwave is electromagnetic wave that vibrates at 1GHz and above. Numerous transmission systems use microwaves including line-of-sight between buildings and across vast distances, communications satellites, PCS cellular systems and wireless LANs. Microwaves were first used to transmit across long distances that were difficult to wire as long as line-of-sight was possible. One advantage with microwave is that communications can be provided to remote areas.

COMPUTER NETWORKS

Using the digital switching technology and different kinds of communication channels as mentioned above wide area computer networks could be developed. Before the invention of digital switching, computer networks could not be extended beyond a single room, building or campus. They were small networks connecting limited number of computers using cables. They are called **local area networks (LANs)**. Only with the invention of digital switching digital data could be carried to long distances using telecommunication lines, which helped the development of **wide area networks (WANs).** When a network cover a metropolitan area it can be called metropolitan area network (MAN). When it cover the whole nation it is called national network. In India, there are number of national computer networks. National Informatics Centre Network (NICNET) and Information and Library Network (INFLIBNET) are examples of national level networks. When a number of networks are connected together it is called internetworking. In internetworking, we can connect between LANs, WANs, National Networks and even individual computers. The internet we use today a product of internetworking.

DIGITAL CONTENT

Although, the digital technology was invented in 1930s, a machine that could store and process digital information was developed only in 1945. The computer was created under the leadership of two electrical engineers – Presper Eckert and John Mauchly. For electric switches they used vacuum tubes or valves. Therefore, ENIAC was very big. It occupied the entire space of a big hall.

Earlier computers were very big and used valves as switches. They were naturally handicapped with lesser memory, processing power and mobility. Transistor was invented in 1956 by a team of three scientists – William Bradford Shockley, John Bardeen and Walter H. Brattain. They shared the Nobel Prize for Physics. Transistors occupied lesser space compared to vacuum tubes and consumed less electricity. With the invention of transistors in 1956, computers became smaller and could process large quantity of data. When compared to present day size of the computer they were bigger computers and known as mainframe computers. Mainframe computers dominated the 1960s and 1970s.

An integrated circuit also referred to as IC, a chip, or a microchip is a set of electronic circuits on one small plate or chip of semiconductor material, usually silicon. This can be made much smaller than an independent circuit. ICs can be made very compact. several billion transistors can be integrated into an area having the size of a fingernail. Integrated circuits are used in all electronic equipment today and have revolutionized the world of electronics. Computers, mobile phones, and other digital home appliances are now very small and handy because of the integrated circuits.

The real revolution in the field of computer happened with the invention of integrated circuit (IC). Computers became smaller and acquired greater speed, memory, and processing power. What is appreciable is that the prices of computers became affordable and the concept of home computer emerged in the late 1970s. Perhaps computer is the only machine becoming smaller, growing in power as the prices are coming down. It is with the development of personal computers and availability of large scale **secondary storage devices**, ***(more about secondary storage divices will be presented along with components of computer)***, digital conversion of documents started in a big way.

When printing was invented by Johan Guttenberg in 1450, all the manuscripts were converted to print form. With the invention of digital technology and digital storage facilities, the conversion of print documents into digital form started in a big way. A very high proportion of the print media has been converted to digital media. High speed scanners are developed to speed up the process of digitization. By a technique known as Optical Character Recognition (OCR) the digitized documents can be converted to editable form. A number of formats like the Portable Document Format (PDF) have been developed for the storage of digitized documents. Also we have a number of software packages like Adobe Acrobat for managing digitized documents.

Robert Noyce

Jack Kilby

Jack Kilby and Robert Noyce invented the Integrated Circuit

The information resources available in the digital format encompass all subjects and all forms of information. Server computers with capacious memory, and the emergence of digital publishing during the 1990s resulted in the explosive growth of digital resources. The digital content is growing every moment. Major digital resources now available include electronic journals, digital libraries, reference sources and bibliographic databases.

During the early 1960s, many of the leading abstracting services started computerized production of abstracting and indexing services with the intension of speeding up of the production of abstracting services. This reduced the gap between publication of journals and their inclusion in the secondary journals. This resulted in the creation of bibliographic databases, which could be stored in the computer and searched for specific information. Using these databases online information retrieval started in 1969. Now thousands of databases are available for online searching.

DIGITAL LIBRARIES

Large scale digital conversion of books and other information sources resulted in the creation of a number of digital libraries. Digital library is a collection of digitized documents. Now there are number of digital libraries in the world. If you want a complete list of digital libraries available in the world, visit *http://www.e-book.com.au/freebooks.htm#2* Some of the major digital libraries are:

1. World Public Library *(http://www.worldpuplic library.org/)*
2. The Internet Public Library *(http://www.ipl.org/)*
3. National Science Digital Library (NSDL) *(http://nsdl.org/)*
4. National Science Digital Library (NSDL) – India *(http://nsdl.niscair.res.in/)*
5. Digital Library of India (DLI) *(http://dli.iiit.ac.in/)*

DIGITAL PUBLISHING OR ELECTRONIC PUBLISHING

Electronic publishing or E-publishing is refers to a type of publishing that does not include printed books. Millions of books are published worldwide in the digital format. Just like we purchase printed books, we can purchase e-books also through e-book sellers. **Amazon.com** is a known e-book seller. For reading e-books these booksellers provide e-book readers also. The e-book reader provided by the Amazon.com is called **Kindle**. E-book sellers are known by the name **E-book aggregators**.

E-JOURNALS

Full text online became a reality in the 1990s. Many current magazines, journals and newspapers are now available online. The first electronic, full-text e-journal including graphics was *Online Journal of Current Clinical Trials* (OJCCT). At present more than 60,000 journals and magazines are published in the digital format and they are accessible through the Internet. E-journals can be subscribed through agents just like we subscribe print journals. EBSCO is a leading agency through whom we can subscribe e-journals.

The foregoing account points to the increasing availability of digital content. The details of digital resources mentioned so far are more related to libraries. There are also number of activities that generate large quantity of digital data. Complete information about the population of India is available in the digital form. The airways and railways reserve seats for thousands of passengers every day, which can be searched from anywhere. Similarly government administration generate large quantity of information as part of the e-governance. The list is not complete. As we depend more on computer and computer networks generation of digitized data is also on the increase. Roughly the digital resources available in the world can be categorized as follows:

- Bibliographic Databases
- Data related to Population, Weather, Economy, Education etc.,
- Administrative data
- Digital Libraries
- Online Book Stores
- Open Access Resources
- E-journals
- Article Citation Services
- Information Portals
- Directories and Reference Books
- Subject Gateways
- Audio and Video on demand
- Software packages
- Games

In this chapter we have learned about all the three components of IT, computer, communication and digital content. Only the basic ideas about these components are given here. With the emergence of global network of networks like the internet, accessing the digital resources has become easier. Through the internet we can not only access data, but also music and videos. It can be said that the Internet is a true example of IT, all components are very efficiently combined. Now let us examine the importance of IT.

IMPORTANCE OF INFORMATION TECHNOLOGY

For nearly six centuries, all the knowledge humanity has acquired had been stored in the print format. Of course, print format is an ideal format and it was carrying forward information from generation to generation. However, we have seen in the beginning of this chapter that the print media started showing limitations in transmitting information. Information transfer required more flexibility and transparency. This is because; information is growing as we go on using it. As a result, information grows at an exponential rate. That is, the existing information doubles at intervals of ten years. To manage information efficiently humanity required more efficient systems of information storage, processing and dissemination. The invention of digital technology, computer and various types of communication channels made it possible to manage information efficiently. It eliminated the barriers of space and time. Any information available anywhere in the world can be accessed from anywhere. A piece of information available in Trivandrum can be accessed from Massachusetts if you have access to a network.

When you reserve a return ticket by train from Delhi to Trivandrum now, you will find your name displayed at the Delhi station when you go to the station for the return journey. This was not possible when we managed things by typing or writing. Also if you want to find out if a person has reserved train or air ticket for a journey you can find out from any point.

Modern computer is a machine that collect, process, store and disseminate information. Library is also a place, where information is collected, processed, stored and disseminated. Today information plays a very important role in our working and everyday lives. It is only because of the availability of computer and computer networks; it became possible to manage information very efficiently. As time goes on dependence on IT for information management will also be on the increase.

Information Technology has influenced every sphere of human life. Booking of tickets for travel, remittance of bills for various public services, audio and visual communications, online commerce, digital music and video on demand, banking, share market, etc have been influenced by IT. Computer memory doubles every two years according to Moore's Law*. If this phenomenon goes unchallenged, a handheld device like a cell phone which can now deal with all information and communication needs will have a minimum storage capacity of 500G by 2020. Such a device can be organized in such a way that it can record everything you hear, see, say and write. Research is going on to develop software that can retrieve the required piece of information from this vast store of information. The total recall research going on in Microsoft will accomplish this task in the near future.

We have understood what is information technology? the progress IT has been making, its impact and its future. IT has become a tool for everybody. Irrespective of the discipline one specializes, everybody has to learn the fundamentals of IT. This is more so for librarians, as he is catering to all learners irrespective of the field of specialization. As he has to apply IT in acquiring, processing and dissemination of information, he should acquire knowledge of IT at some more depth than an ordinary person. Therefore, let us now learn more about computer, computer software and computer networks.

2
THE COMPUTER

INTRODUCTION

From symbolic gestures of the primitive society to virtual reality communication systems of modern society, humanity has traveled a long distance. Information is the life blood of human development. We have seen that the growth of information is the most important problem faced by the information managers. The quantity and variety of information and specific user needs pose serious challenges in the storage, processing and retrieval of information. Humanity has been evolving newer techniques to make information processing and retrieval more flexible and transparent. Milestones in this direction are invention of paper in 100 AD, invention of the movable press in 1450, and invention of the binary system for the machine storage and processing of information.

In the previous chapter we had learned how the binary system was evolved. Each digit in the binary system either 0 or 1 is called a bit. A unit of 8 bits (binary digits) is called a byte (bits by eight). A byte is used to represent a character (Letter, digit or symbol). For example, the letter '**A**' in the English alphabet is represented by the byte '01000001' and '**B**' is represented by the byte '01000011'. Similarly the number '1' is represented by the byte '11110001' and number '2' is represented by the byte '11110010'. In this manner every bit of information can be represented digitally. There are international standards, which specify binary equivalent of letters, digits and other units of information. The two international standards, which specify 8 bit equivalent of letters and digits, are the 'EBCDIC' (Extended Binary Coded Decimal Interchange) and ASCII (American Standards Code for Information Interchange). ASCII is more popular compared to EBCDIC. Initially, when the digital technology was invented, only digits, letters, and symbols could be represented digitally. Later technologies have been evolved for converting audio, graphics, and video into the digital format. Thus computers became capable to handle multimedia content. Another revolutionary step was the invention of hypertext and hypermedia techniques for linking related information within the computer or network.

The form and functions of computers have been evolving for the last seven decades. First generation computers were used mainly for calculations or computations. That is how the name computer evolved. Suppose if a name is given now for this all in one machine it would have been different. A modern computer is collecting, processing, storing and disseminating information. Thus a modern computer can be defined as *"a machine that accept, process, store, and disseminate information."*

EVOLUTION OF COMPUTERS

As the system of binary representation of information became possible, search began to develop a machine that could store binary information. In the previous chapter we have learned that ENIAC (Electronic Numeric Integrator and Calculator) was developed in 1945 to store binary information. From ENIAC to the present day computers the evolution was fast and astonishing. The progress made during the last seven decades in the field of computer science is unparallel as no other area of science has shown growth as the field of computer science has achieved. Early computers were used only for computing or mathematical operations. That was why the machines that handled binary digits were called computers. Now computers are doing lesser mathematical operations, they are now mainly used for information processing.

Drastic changes have taken place in the form, function, speed and size of computers. Not only computers, computer accessories like recording devices and printers have also undergone tremendous changes. Now we have a variety of computers: mainframes, mini computers, personal computers, lap tops, tablets, palm tops, etc. The concept of home computer emerged by the mid 1970s. Before that computers were used only in large institutions like universities and government departments. With the development of home computers or Personal Computers (PC), computers became cheaper and affordable. This is one of the reasons for the popularization of information technology. Now everybody has at least seen a computer. We reserve our tickets for travel by train or plane using computer networks, we pay our bills through computer networks, we can ascertain the availability of seats in trains and planes and we can even book our tickets by sitting at home.

Let us examine in some more details the development of computer, its characteristics and varied uses. The computers we see today are not like the ones, which existed some six or seven decades ago. During the 1950s and 60s, a whole building was required to install a computer system, which worked on vacuum tubes. People could not even think, if it could be possible to keep a computer on the tabletop or carry one when a person is traveling. Now you can keep a computer on your table, you can travel with a laptop or tablet computer. There are also computers that you can keep in your pocket. As the computers are becoming smaller, its power is increasing. Now a small pocket calculator is 1000 times more powerful than the ENIAC. The reasons for the reduction in the size and increase in the processing power and speed are attributed to the discovery of transistors and their integration into microprocessors.

GENERATIONS OF COMPUTERS

As newer technologies emerged in the field of electronics, computers acquired more power and versatility. Computers became smaller, as it acquired more power. Considering the features of computers from time to time computers are categorized into generations. The main features considered are the type of switches used, processing speed, processing power, operating system and storage capability. Let us examine the features of computers belonging to each generation.

FIRST GENERATION COMPUTERS

We have seen that the first computer ENIAC was developed in the year 1945. This computer was developed by a team of engineers at the University of Pennsylvania in USA. In spite of its huge size, weight and high power consumption, the computer could store only 80 bytes of information. This small memory was used mainly for mathematical calculations. When you want to change the mode, that is, from 'addition' to 'multiplication', you had to change the cables in the computer manually. This was very time consuming and difficult. A solution to this problem was developed by storing a logical set of instructions called program inside the computer memory. This automatically changed from one function to the other. This was the first use of program in a computer. **John Von Newman** developed the practice of stored programme in 1946. Even today this technique is used in computers and it is known as **Newman architecture**.

Commercial production of electronic computers with

stored program began in early 1950s. One of the early computers of this type was UNIVAC-1 built by the Univac division of Remington Rand. All computers, which used vacuum tube for electronic circuits come under the category of I Generation. As each vacuum tube consumed half watt of electricity, the first generation computers consumed as much electricity as required for running a train. Consequently it generated high degree of heat, which prevented continuous functioning. For first generation computers, programming was initially done using machine language. Assembly language was invented in the early fifties to use in these computers. It is needless to say that these computers were very costly and the recurring expenses to maintain these computers were also unaffordable to most of the institutions. Therefore, uses of these computers were confined only to scientific and engineering establishments. Now First generation computers are used only for display IT museums.

SECOND GENERATION COMPUTERS

A big revolution in electronics took place with the invention of transistors. William Bradford Shockley along with John Bardeen and Walter H. Brattain had won the Nobel prize for this invention in 1956. Transistors occupied lesser space and used only a tenth of the power required by vacuum tubes. They also could switch from '0' to '1' state in a few microseconds, about a tenth of the time needed by tubes. Thus switching circuits for computers made with transistors were about ten times more reliable, ten times faster, consumed one tenth of the power, occupied only one tenth of the space and cost one tenth of the first generation computers. This generation of computers lasted till the mid 1960s.

Other characteristics of the second generation computers were invention of the magnetic core for storage of data. Magnetic core memory was used to store large quantities of data with random access facility. The memory capacity of the second generation computers was about 100 Kilo Bytes. Magnetic disk storage was another characteristic of the second generation computer. Higher reliability and availability of large memory availability led to the development of high level languages. FORTRAN, COBOL, Algol and SNOBOL were developed during the second generation. With higher speed CPUs and the advent of magnetic tape and disk storage, operating systems were developed. Good batch operating systems particularly the ones on the IBM 7000 series computers emerged during the second generation. Computers were largely used for business purpose and major applications were payroll, inventory control, marketing and production planning. It was during the second generation new professions such as systems analysts and programmers emerged.

THIRD GENERATION OF COMPUTERS

The third generation began in 1965 with germanium transistors being replaced by silicon transistors. With the development of integrated circuits (IC) computers could be still smaller. IC, as the name indicates, is the integration of a number of transistors on non conducting media. Initially only a very limited number of transistors were integrated on to a silicon chip. From small-scale integrated circuits, this had about 10 transistors per chip. Switching speed of transistors and reliability went up 10 times and computer size also came down by a factor of 10. The cumulative effect of all these factors was the emergence of extremely powerful CPUs with the capacity to carry out one million instructions per second. The size of memories reached up to 4 MB. Magnetic disk technology improved considerably and hard disk capacity reached 100 MB. The combined effect of all these factors led to the development of shared operating system which ultimately let to the development of computer networks, client-server computing, database management systems and online services.

Computer languages like FORTRAN and COBOL were improved to suit the third generation computers. The new versions were named FORTRAN IV and COBOL 68. In addition, the PL/1 programming language of IBM emerged as a powerful computer language. Probably the third generation ended by 1975. Even with the emergence of third generation computers, it could not become popular. The use of computers was restricted to institutions. Although prices came down it did not reach a level that individuals could afford.

FOURTH GENERATION COMPUTERS - FIRST PHASE

The fourth generation can be described under two phases. The first phase is a decade between 1976 and 1985, which was marked by the emergence of microprocessor chip. Medium scale integrated circuits, large scale integrated circuits and very large scale integrated circuits (VLSI) were developed. In VLSI 50000 transistors could be integrated into one chip. The emergence of the microprocessor led to two directions in computer development – the emergence of extremely powerful personal computers and drastic reduction in computer prices. The emergence of Personal Computer (PC) was the most important development that marked the fourth generation computers. Another important development was independent development of computer software – both operating systems and application programs. A new company called Microsoft developed the operating system called the MS-DOS (Microsoft Disk Operating System) . The open architecture of IBM PC allowed many small companies manufacture PCs compatible with IBM PCs, which were called IBM clones. The appearance of the PCs drastically changed in 1977 when Steve Jobs and Steve Wozniak developed the Apple II PC.

During the first phase of the fourth generation MS DOS became the *defacto* standard for all IBM PC and its clones. Networks of computers and distributed computer systems were developed during this period. Disk memories increased up to 1000 MB. A significant development during this period was the development of several advanced programming languages and operating systems. The cost of computer became affordable to individuals. Computing became cheap and people all over the world started using computer.

FOURTH GENERATION COMPUTERS - SECOND PHASE

A span of 15 years from 1986 to 2000 can be considered as the second phase of the fourth generation. This period saw the relentless increase in the speed of microprocessors and the size of main memory. The speed of the computer and the size of the computer memory increased exponentially. The speed of the computer and the number of circuits integrated into the microchip doubled every two years. Gordon Moore the cofounder of the Intel Corporation predicted that the phenomenon of exponential growth, i.e., doubling the speed every 24 months will continue infinitely. So far Moore's prediction has not been disproved. Therefore, it is called the **Moore's law**. Most of the features of the mainframe computers, which dominated during the second generation, could be done using personal computers.

In the secondary storage devices also lots of improvements took place during this period. Hard disk capacity of ordinary PC went up to 500GB during this period. Optical storage devices like CD-ROM and DVD were developed during this phase. The use of magnetic tape as a secondary storage medium became uncommon.

Computer networks were perfected during this period. With the development of digital communication systems it became possible to build wide area networks, national and international networks and network of networks. Library automation, networking of libraries, computerized information storage and retrieval, electronic publishing online information retrieval and publication of online journals were some of the achievement in the area of information management.

A number of programming languages and programs became popular during this period. Programming languages like C, C++, PROLOG, and operating systems like the Windows and application programs like MS Office, photo editing software, games, accounting software and a number of authoring software emerged during this period. Use of HTML for achieving the hypertext and hypermedia capabilities in communication was another important development during the second phase of IV generation computers.

Availability of computers at affordable cost, popularization of several user-friendly software packages, operation of computers using graphical user interfaces (GUI) and use of computer and computer networks for a number of public services like ticket reservation, online access of general and scholarly information and electronic commerce through the Internet made computer use very common and computer became an essential tool for every house.

The introduction of www as an Internet interface in 1991, brought in hypertext and hypermedia capabilities. The launching of graphical Internet browser, the Navigator and Communicator in 1994 by the Netscape company and later the Internet Browser in1996 by the Microsoft made Internet use very easy and popular. Increase in the digital content of the Internet in the form of digital libraries, e-journals, and information gateways made the Internet a very essential facility for students, teachers and scholars.

Table summarizing features of computers in generations

Generation	Years	Switching device	Storage device	Software	Main applications
First	1946 – 1955	Vacuum tubes	Acoustic delay lines and later magnetic drum. 1KB memory	Machine and assembly languages. Simple monitors	Mostly scientific. Later simple business systems
Second	1956 – 1965	Transistors	Magnetic core main memory. Tape and disk peripheral memory. Main Memory 100 KB	High-level languages. FORTRAN, COBOL, Algol, Batch Operating Systems	Extensive Business Applications. Engineering design and Research
Third	1966 – 1975	Integrated Circuits (IC)	High speed magnetic cores. Large 100 MB disks. 1 MB Main memory	FORTRAN IV, COBOL 68, PL/1 time shared O. S.	Database management systems. Online systems
Fourth – First phase	1975 – 1984	Large scale IC, (LSI) Micro-processors	Semiconductor memory, Winchester disk. 100 MB Mem. 1000 MB Disks	FORTRAN 77, Pascal, Ada, COBOL - 74	Personal computers. Distributed systems. Integrated CAD/CAM
Fourth – Second phase	1985 - 2000	Very Large Scale IC. Over 100 million Transistors	Semiconductor memory. 1GB main memory. 100 GB disk	C, C++, JAVA, PROLOG, FORTRAN, GUI systems. Internet	Simulation, Visualization, Parallel computing, Networking, Virtual reality and Multimedia
Fifth	2001+	Very large Scale IC	Memory 5GB + 500 GB HD	Artificial intelligence	Instructional programming

FIFTH GENERATION COMPUTERS

Towards the end of the fourth generation, efforts were on to create a computer architecture different from Von Nemann architecture with the ultimate goal of producing computers with artificial intelligence. Such computers should be able to produce programs on the basis of specifications of requirements or specifications oriented programming. The research towards this direction was taken under the leadership of Japan, USA, Europe and India. However, there could not be any revolutionary change in the computer architecture. The fifth generation is also marked by the availability of online multimedia content like real time music and video.

During this period increase in the number of transistors integrated into one chip went on significantly. Pentium 4 processors integrate nearly 60 million transistors in a single chip. It is expected that by the turn of the next decade, the number may increase to 100 million. Anyway, thinking computer is a distant dream.

TYPES OF COMPUTERS

When discussing generations of computers, it could be seen that computers differed mainly by the type of circuits each generation made use of. First generation computers made use of valves, second generation computers made use of transistors and from third generation onwards made use of ICs. When look at the type of computers the criteria considered are mainly size, speed storage capacity, processing power and kind of use. According to these criteria, computers are categorized into the following types:

PALM PCS/SIMPUTERS

Computers with capabilities nearly that of PCs which can be held in a palm have emerged. Palm accepts handwritten inputs using an electronic pen, which can be used to write on a Palm's screen (besides a tiny keyboard). It has small disk storage and can be connected to a wireless network. One has to train the system on the user's handwriting before it can be used. A Palm computer also has facilities to use as a mobile phone, fax and email machine. A version of he MS operating system called Windows-CE is available for palm.

An Indian initiative to meet the need of rural population of developing countries is called Simputer. This is a mobile handheld computer with input through icons on a touch sensitive LCD display panel. A unique feature of Simputer is the use of free open source OS, called GNU/Linux. The cost of simputer is low as there is no cost for the OS.

PERSONAL COMPUTERS (PCS)

First generation computers were just demonstrating the possibility of machine storage of information. People at that time did not expect that computers will ever be used at home for personal use. Computers were very big machines and stored only a small quantity of information. It was only in the 1970s that the idea of home computer emerged as machines that could be used at home. The prototype of personal computer was **Altair** developed by Ed Roberts an engineer who owned a calculator company called MITS. That was only a squire box with a row of buttons on one side, called operating panel. Data were given to the computer using this panel. The present shape of a personal computer with a keyboard, display monitor

Altair Developed at MITS in 1974

Apple I April 1, 1976

and central processing unit or CPU was decided by Steve Jobs and Steve Wozniyak founders of the Apple Computers Inc.

The most popular PCs are desktop machines. The personal computers made by IBM are called IBM PC. PCs manufactured by other companies on IBM standard are called IBM compatible PCs. IBM and IBM compatible PCs mostly use Windows, Windows XP or GNU/Linux as OS. The memory of PCs has grown up to 5G and the normal capacity of the hard disk is 500 GB. PCs are now provided with floppy drive, CD or DVD read/write drive (also called combo-drive), and a number of parallel and serial ports for connectivity to accessories and networks. Now PCs are provided with Universal Serial Ports (USB) for connection to various devices like printer, camera and speakers and copying content to flash memory device called pen drive. The use of black and white monitors have become very uncommon. Color monitors based on CRT display or flat panel display using LCD or Plasma have become common place.

Another company called Apple also manufactures PCs. Apple PCs are known as Apple Macintosh. In fact Apple first demonstrated the present form of a PC consisting of keyboard, CPU and monitor.

WORKSTATIONS

Workstations are also desktop machines. They are however, more powerful providing processor speeds about 10 times that of PCs. Most workstations have a large color video display unit. Normally they have main memory ranging from 5 MB to 20GB and hard disk ranging from 1000G to 5000G. High quality graphics facilities and large video screens are provided in most of the workstations. Workstations are used to execute numeric and graphic intensive applications.

SERVER COMPUTERS

Servers are computers with large memory, and secondary storage facility. They are used for specific purposes such as high performance numerical computing, web page hosting, database storage, online information service, printing, etc. for which large interactive screens are not necessary. At the same time computers used as servers have high performance processors, and large main memory. Database servers have big online disk storage. Print servers support several high-speed printers.

Servers are parts of networks. Each server performs a variety of services to satisfy the needs of clients. The name of the server is based on the task it is carrying out. Thus we have printer server, file server, email server, news group server, database server, Internet server, etc. Different types of servers can exist in a network. Most common types of servers are File server, Mail server, Internet server and so on.

MAINFRAME COMPUTERS

Mainframe computers are large computer systems. During the 1960s and 70s, all computers were called mainframes. There are small, medium and large-scale mainframes, handling from a handful to tens of thousands of online terminals. Large-scale mainframes support hundreds of gigabytes of main memory and terabytes of disk storage.

Until the emergence of the personal computers in the early 1980s, computers were large, and consisted of multiple cabinets. These computers required special room conditions, and specially trained staff and programmers. Large mainframe computers required the entire area of bigger rooms for their installation and functioning. These computers were used to fulfill the computing needs of large companies, corporations, and telecommunication systems. They are very powerful and huge with large memory and very high processing power.

MINICOMPUTERS

A medium-scale, centralized computer that functioned as a multi-user system is called minicomputers. With the emergence of powerful personal computers, the need for minicomputers diminished. The minicomputer was developed to serve the computing needs of smaller companies and academic institutions. The minicomputer, also known as midrange computer, has essentially the same functionality of the mainframe computers but on a smaller scale. The minicomputer was developed largely to open new market for computers, as only large establishments could afford for large mainframes. Now minicomputers completely disappeared from market.

SUPERCOMPUTERS

Supercomputers are the fastest of computers available at any given time. They are extremely powerful computers used mostly in research; and space missions, military and governmental applications. A supercomputer which can cost crores of rupees combines the processing speed of thousands of personal computers to solve very large and complex problems in hours or days which otherwise would have taken weeks, months or years. Some of the uses of super computers are: numerical weather prediction, designing supersonic aircrafts, design of rockets and space stations, etc.

MOBILE COMPUTER DEVICES

Mobile computer devices includes laptop computers, notebook computers, tablet computers, PDAs, smart phones, iPhones, e-book readers and portable data terminals. They are now in the hands of hundreds of millions of people worldwide. The proliferation of mobile computer devices, and the number of places where they can be used, will increase the number of online information users. One who possesses a mobile computer device can access information from the internet.

A mobile phone is not a mobile computer device unless it includes a Web browser and has the capacity to download and store files.

TYPES OF MOBILE COMPUTER DEVICES

There are six major types of mobile computer devices: laptop computers, notebook computers, tablet computers, PDAs, smart phones, and portable data terminals. The first three are often called "portable" computers and the second three are often called "hand-held" computers. Each is briefly discussed in the following paragraphs.

LAPTOP COMPUTERS

Laptop computers are sometimes called "desktop replacement PCs," offer desktop PC performance in a mobile environment. They have been widely available in North America since 2002. The typical laptop has a 14 to 17 inch screen; internal DVD-ROM or DVD-RW drive (combo drive); large full-featured keyboard; integrated modem, network, Bluetooth, and Wi-Fi capabilities; high quality integrated audio and speaker system; three or more hours of battery life, low battery consumption; and the capability to be upgraded. Despite their power, they weigh only three to twelve pounds each. Many laptops have not only a built-in keyboard, but also a touchpad or pointing stick for input. A mouse can usually be attached. Despite these advantages of laptop computers, desktop PCs continue to be very popular because they are more durable and less costly to own over a period of several years. The price of laptops used to be four or five times more compared to the price of desktop PCs. Now the prices of laptops are coming down to just double the price of an ordinary PC.

NOTEBOOK COMPUTERS

Notebook computers are lightweight computers that have a very thin profile; 12 to 14-inch screen; no internal DVD or CD system, no internal floppy drive; limited graphics capabilities; integrated modem and network connection; small keyboard; low power consumption; and four or more hours of battery life. Upgradeability is usually limited. The typical notebook computers weigh around 1.5 to three pounds. While sometimes not differentiated from a laptop computer, the former is larger, more powerful, and much closer to a desktop PC.

TABLET PCs

Tablet computers are slate-shaped mobile computers equipped with a touch screen or graphics tablet/screen hybrid. This allows the user to operate the computer with a stylus, digital pen, or fingertip, instead of a keyboard or a mouse. However, an external keyboard or mouse can be attached. The stylus also can be used to type on a pen-based key layout. Some tablet PCs also support voice recognition. The screen is usually small, often as little as eight inches. Tablets offer half the processor speed and memory of notebook computers, but the resolution is comparable and the weight is less than half that of notebook computers.

PDAs

The PDAs (Personal Digital Assistants) have been among the most popular type of hand-held mobile computer devices since 2000. Initially they were used for keeping track of schedules, maintaining directories of names and addresses, and accessing e-mail. Only since 2003 it was upgraded with more processor speeds and memories. PDAs with a Web browser, cellular telephone, and fax capabilities were available. When cell phone manufacturers started producing smart phones, PDAs have become outmoded and now-a-days nobody use it.

SMART-PHONES

Smart-phones are a compromise between a PDA and a cellular phone, with a focus on the cellular phone part. A smart-phone allows a user to install programs, store information, and undertake e-mail and web browsing. There are no industry standards for defining what is a smart-phone, therefore, any mobile device that has more than basic cell phone capability may be called a smart-phone. The operating systems used in different smart phones are: Google's Android, Apple's iOS, Nokia's Symbian, RIM's BlackBerry OS, Samsung's Bada, Microsoft's Windows Phone and Hewlett-Packard's webOS

iPOD

iPod is a brand of portable media players designed and marketed by Apple Computer launched in 2001. Devices in the iPod range are primarily music players, designed around a central scroll wheel. The full-sized model stores media on an internal hard drive, while the smaller iPod **nano** and **iPod shuffle** use flash memory. Like many digital audio players, iPods can also serve as external data storage devices.

iPAD

The **iPad** is a series of tablet computers designed and marketed by Apple Inc., which runs Apple's iOS. The first iPad was released on April 3, 2010. The most recent iPad models, and iPad Mini, were released on 2012. The user interface is through the device's multi-touch screen, including a virtual keyboard. The iPad has built-in Wi-Fi. Some models have cellular connectivity. An iPad can shoot video, take photos, play music, and perform Internet functions such as web-browsing and emailing. Other functions include games, GPS navigation and social networking. According to Steve Jobs, the cofounder of Apple Inc. "our strategy is really simple. What we want to do is we want to put an incredibly great computer in a book that you can carry around with you and learn how to use it in 20 minutes"

Steve Jobs cofounder of Apple Inc. and who is responsible for Apple PC, iPad, iPod and iPhone.

iPHONE

The iPhone is a series of smart phones designed and marketed by Apple Inc. It runs Apple's iOS mobile operating system, known as the "iPhone OS". The first generation iPhone was released on June 29, 2007 and the most recent iPhone, the sixth-generation iPhone 5, on September 21, 2012. The user interface is built around the device's multi-touch screen, including a virtual keyboard. The iPhone has Wi-Fi and cellular connectivity (2G, 3G, and 4G).

An iPhone can shoot video, take photos, play music, send and receive email, browse the web, send texts, and receive visual voicemail. Other functions include games, reference, GPS navigation and social networking.

E-BOOK READERS

An **e-book reader**, also called an **e-book device** or **e-reader**, is a device used to display e-books. It may be a device specifically designed for that purpose, or one intended for other purposes as well. The main advantages of these devices are portability, readability of their screens in bright sunlight, and long battery life. The display in e-book reader is by electronic ink, which last longer. Any Personal Data Assistant (PDA) capable of displaying text on a screen and iPads are also used as e-book readers, but without the advantages of an electronic ink display. Amazon.com, Sony and several companies including DC Books Kottayam also manufacture e-book readers.

EMBEDDED COMPUTERS

Virtually all electronic gadgets have a computer built into them in some way. These very small and single purpose processors are classified as embedded computers. An embedded computer is build into another device to control, monitor, or manage some activity of the device. One or more embedded computers do the controls of a microwave oven, automatic washing machine, aircraft, photocopying machine, CT scanners, etc.

3

Basic Hardware

COMPONENTS OF COMPUTER

Basically computer consists of two parts: **hardware** and **software**. For both words singular and plural are the same. Computer hardware and software cannot function independently. A computer can function and perform its functions only with the help of software. Software is instructions to the computer for the functioning of the computer and for doing specific activities. The first person who used a set of instructions as an interface to automatically select various functions of the computer is John Von Newman. Even today the technique is called **Newman Architecture.**

Computer hardware is the collection of physical elements that constitute a computer system. Computer hardware refers to the physical parts or components of a computer such as monitor, keyboard, data storage devices, hard disk, disk drives, mouse and CPU. All are physical objects that you can actually touch. In contrast, software is untouchable. Software exists only as ideas, concepts and symbols. It has no concrete body. A combination of hardware and software forms a usable computing system. There are two types of software – Operating Systems (OS) or System Software and application software.

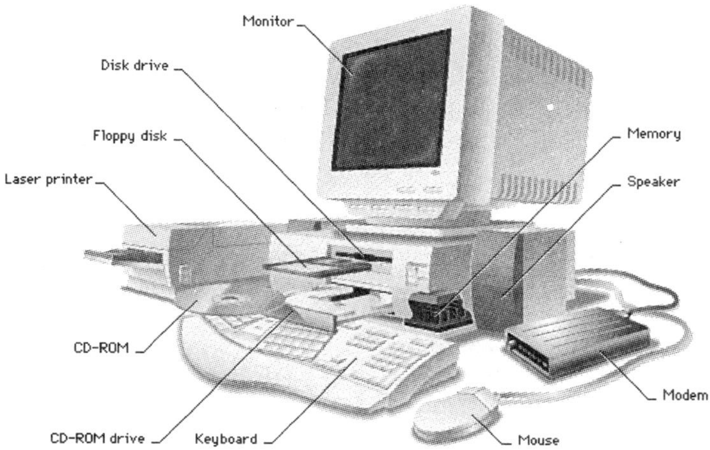

A Computer System

The computer is operated with the help of the Operating System and the computer performs various functions with the help of application software. MS Windows is an example for operating system and MS Word is an example for application program.

WHAT IS COMPUTER HARDWARE?

Hardware as mentioned in the previous paragraph constitutes the physical parts of the computer. Hardware components are basically three types. Input hardware, output hardware and processing hardware. In the case of computer networks there is one more component – the transmission lines. The hardware design specifies the commands it can follow, and the instructions (the software) tell it what to do.

Input, output, storage, processing and Transmission are the main functions of hardware. Computer's storage capability, speed of processing, transmission, etc., are determined by the hardware. The hardware requirement is based on the size of the information to be stored and processed. The computer system consisting of computer the machine and its accessories constitute the hardware, that is, the physical parts of a computer.

INPUT DEVICES

The parts of the computer and devices used for giving information to the computer for processing are called the input hardware. The keyboard, mouse, scanner, digital camera, microphone, etc. come under this category.

KEYBOARD

Keyboard is the component, which forms an integral part of the computer and used not only for data input, but also for data output. Therefore the keyboard is an input-output device, whereas, a printer is only an output device. Keyboard is the most commonly used input device. The computer keyboards are also designed on the basis of the typewriter keyboard. But a computer keyboard has a number of additional keys for performing predefined functions. The Escape [Esc] key, Function keys that are located on the upper part of the keyboard, Page Up [Pg up], Page Down [Pg Dn], Delete, Home, End, and Numerical Key pad are some of the extra keys available on the computer keyboard. There are also other keys like key for Internet and Windows. Although, there are minor variations in the layout of keys and shape of keyboards, the basic keys and functions are the same. In laptops and tablet PCs the keyboard is a built in facility.

The first six letters on the left hand side of the upper row reads 'QWERTY'. The keyboards beginning with QWERTY on the upper row are called QWERTY keyboards. A number of alternatives have been tried in an effort to make the keyboards more convenient and faster. However, QWERTY keyboards are commonly used as they are more traditional and typewriter and computer users are more familiar with it.

FUNCTION KEYS

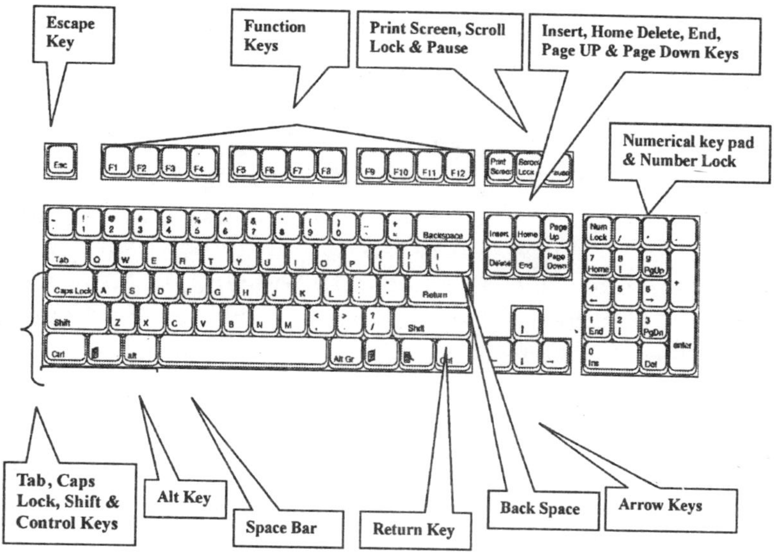

Computer Keyboard

Important keys in a computer keyboard are as detailed below:

Enter (return) key : In text applications, it ends a paragraph or short line. In data applications, it signals the end of the input for that field or line.

Cursor keys : The four arrow keys move the cursor on screen. They are used in conjunction with shift, alt and control to move the cursor in bigger jumps; for example,

Control Up Arrow might scroll the screen. Some earlier keyboards didn't have cursor keys, in which case, control or alt was used with some letter keys.

Numeric lock : Locks the keypad. By pressing the key again the numeric keypad is opened.

Home & End keys : Commonly used to move the cursor to the extreme left or right side of the current line. Often used in conjunction with shift, control and alt. For example, control-home take the cursor to the beginning of a text file and control-end move the cursor to the end of a text file. This can make the text editing faster.

Page up/Page down keys : Used to move the cursor up and down a page, screen or frame. Often used in combination with shift, control and alt.

Function keys : Used to display a menu or perform a specific function, they are located in a cluster on the left side or in a row across the top of the keyboard (F1, F2, etc.). They are often used with the shift, control and alt keys to extend the number of options. Software developers can specify the functions of these keys.

Backspace key : Used to delete the character to the left of the cursor and may be used with the shift, control and alt keys to erase segments of text. This is an extra-wide, typewriter-style key.

Delete key : Used to erase the character at the current cursor location. Used in conjunction with the shift, control and alt keys, it is used to erase any segment of text, such as a word, sentence or paragraph.

Insert key : Insert key toggles between insert and overwrite mode. Also it is used to "paste" a segment of text or graphics into the document at the current cursor location.

Repeating keys : Most computer keys repeat when hold down, a phenomenon first-time computer users must get used to. If you hold a key down that is used to command the computer, you'll be entering the character repeatedly.

Control, Alt, command & option keys : Used like a shift key, these keys are held down while another key is pressed to command the computer in a variety of ways.

Escape key : Commonly used to exit or cancel the current mode such as exiting from a menu. Also used to clear an area or repeat a function such as redrawing the screen. If you hold a key down that is used to command the computer, you will be entering the command several times.

POINTING DEVICES

A number of pointing devices are used for inputting data. Pointing devices are used particularly in a GUI* environment. The important pointing devices for inputting data are mouse, trackballs, pointing sticks, and touch pads. **Mouse** and **touch pads** are commonly used.

Mouse: The use of mouse with computer has become very common. A mouse is a device that is rolled about on a desktop and directs a pointer on the computer's display screen. The mouse pointer is the symbol that indicates the position of the mouse on the display screen. It may be an arrow, a rectangle, a + sign, the shape of the letter 'I' or it can take the shape of a persons pointing finger. When it takes the shape of I or **'I beam'** as it is called, the computer is ready to accept text. When the mouse reaches a hyperlink immediately it attains the shape of a pointing finger. When a graphic task like drawing a rectangle, line, or circle is selected, the cursor changes into a + sign. Practice the use of mouse by selecting various tasks and watch the change of shapes of cursor.

The mouse is connected to the computer with the help of a cable attached to the special port of the CPU. The tail like cord and the rounded head of the device earned its name ***mouse.***

There are two to four buttons in a mouse the left button is used to select, highlight, drag or insert. The functions of the other buttons vary from software to software. In some mouse there is a middle button that helps to scroll the contents inside a Window. This button is called scroll button or scroll wheel.

The mouse is connected to the computer with the help of a cable attached to the special port of the CPU.

The tail like cord and the rounded head of the device earned its name ***mouse.*** Basically there are three types of mice :

- **Mechanical mouse :** This is the older style of mouse. This was first used with early Apple Macintosh PCs. In a mechanical mouse, the movement of a rubber ball when it is moved against a rough surface causes movement of the cursor on the screen.
- **Optical mouse :** The optical mouse eliminates the use of moving rubber ball and uses optical scanning to detect the movement of the mouse over virtually any surface (except reflecting surfaces like glass)

RIGHT BUTTON

There are two or three buttons in a mouse the left button is used to select, highlight, drag or insert. The functions of the other buttons vary from software to software. In some mouse there is a middle button that help to scroll the contents inside a Window. This button is called scroll button or scroll wheel.

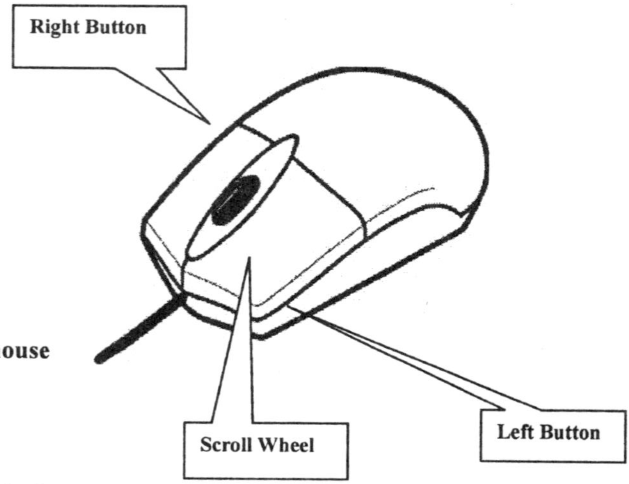

A scroll mouse

GUI stands for graphical user interface. In GUI we operate computer by clicking graphical representations of programs called Icons. First developed by Xerox Corporation and implemented first in Apple Macintoshcomputer.

TOUCH PAD

The touch pad is a small flat surface on which you slide your finger. As you move your finger, the cursor follows the movement. You click by tapping your finger on the pad's surface or by pressing buttons positioned in front of the pad. Touch pads are common on portable computers and positioned just below the space bar.

SCANNER, AUDIO, VIDEO AND PHOTOGRAPHIC INPUT

Data can be input to the computer by transferring from the source. You don't have to type for data entry. Source data-entry devices such as, scanning devices, barcode readers, character recognition devices, fax machines and imaging systems are used for data input.

SCANNING DEVICES AND BAR-CODE READERS/ SCANNERS

Scanners use laser beams and reflected light to translate images of text, drawings, photos, and the like into digital form. The images can then be processed by a computer, displayed on a monitor, stored on a storage device, or communicated to another computer. Scanners are very essential for creating digital libraries from older and rare documents. It is practically impossible to type the text of old documents for creating the digital library of older documents. Scanners are of different types.

FLATBED IMAGE SCANNERS

A scanner that provides a flat, glass surface to hold pages of paper, books and other objects for scanning. Flatbed image scanners can scan all sorts of documents, even books. They are used for scanning high-quality graphics. In ordinary flatbed scanners, the scanning light moves below the page scanned. There also scanners which scans pages by exposing to light from above. Such scanners are called planetary scanners. These are high-speed scanners, which can scan thousands of pages per day.

HANDHELD SCANNER

It is a scanner that is moved across the image to be scanned by hand. Handheld scanners are small and less expensive than their desktop counterparts, but rely on the skill of the user to move the device across paper.

BARCODE READERS

Scanning devices include barcode readers. A vertical zebra striped marks you see on books and most of the manufactured goods are called bard-codes. Here a value is converted in to a pattern of lines, which can be read using a barcode reader. Using a barcode reader we can prepare bills, list of books etc without the need for typing.

A bar-code

OUTPUT DEVICES

There are two types of output from a computer: Softcopy output and hardcopy output. **Softcopy output** refers to data that is shown on a display screen or when the output is in the form of digital text or graphic, audio and video. **Hardcopy output** refers to printed output. Examples of hard copy outputs are: printouts, text or graphics, from printers. Film, including microfilm and microfiche, are also considered hardcopy output.

COMPUTER MONITORS

Computer monitor is an input/output device. The information we give to the computer and the information we take out of it can be seen on the computer display screen or monitor.

CATHODE RAY TUBE (CRT) DISPLY

Earlier, computer display was by using the **Cathode Ray Tube (CRT). CRT** is a vacuum tube used as a display screen in computer or TV. In fact, the first computer monitor was by adapting a television. CRT monitors are big, produce lot of heat and consume more electricity. Now-a-days, CRT displays are rarely used. During the 1970s and 80s monochrome or black and white monitors were commonly used. Now such monitors have become outdated. Only color monitors are used now.

FLAT PANEL DISPLAY

A thin display screen that uses LCD (Liquid Crystal Display), LED (Light Emitting Diode), etc. Traditionally used in laptops, flat panel displays are commonly used in all types of monitors. With their low power consumption, low radiation and space-saving qualities, flat panels have become the standard.

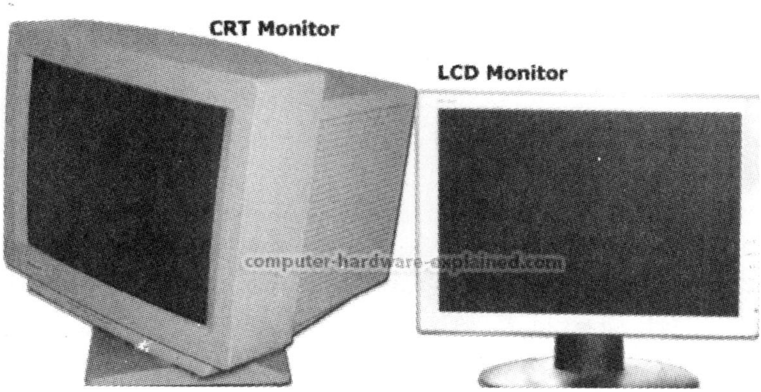

OUTPUT HARDWARE: PRINTERS, PLOTTERS, ETC.

There are number of devices for obtaining hardcopy output from the computer the most important hardcopy output device is the printer.

PRINTERS

Printer is a device that converts computer output into printed images. Basically there are two types of printers: impact printers and non-impact printers.

Impact printer: A printer that uses a printing mechanism that bangs the character image into the ribbon and onto the paper. A dot-matrix printer is an impact printer. Impact printers make sound while printing. A dot-matrix printer is an impact printer. In a library, an impact printer is a nuisance as it makes disturbing sound.

A dot-matrix printer

Non-impact printer: A printer that prints without banging a ribbon onto paper. Laser, LED, ink jet, solid ink, thermal wax transfer and dye sublimation printers are examples of non-impact printers. A non impact printer does not produce any sound while printing.

Low-end laser printers print in the 4 to 8 page per minute (ppm) range. Hewlet-Pakard (HP) is the major manufacturer of printers. Many other companies such as Lexmark, IBM and Canon, Kodak and Minolta manufacture laser printers. There are also laser printers, which combine fax, and photocopying along with printing.

Color laser printers are slower and more costly. For normal printing requirements color laser printers are not necessary. Color inkjet printers do not cost much but their ink cartridges are very costly and unaffordable for individual users. There are also high speed laser printers, which can print more than 100 copies per minute. Such printers are used in big establishments and offices.

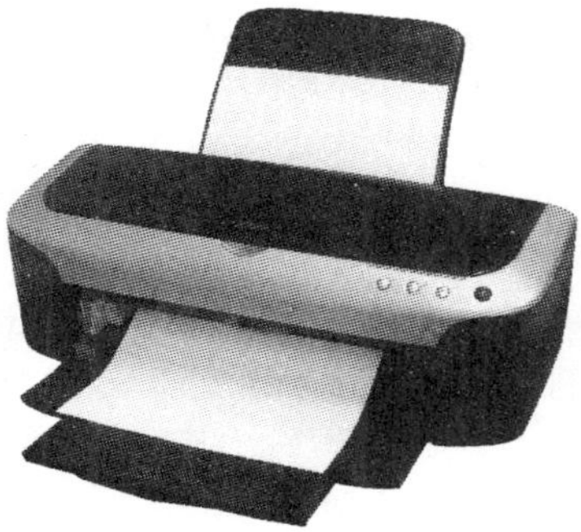

Inkjet Printer

Laser Printer

THERMAL PRINTER

A low- to medium-resolution printer that uses a type of coated paper that darkens when heat is applied to it. The paper is passed by a line of heating elements that burn dots onto the paper. This is typically used as barcode printers and other small specialty printers. It was widely used in early fax machines.

DIGITAL CAMERA

A **digital camera** is a camera that takes video or still photographs, or both, digitally by recording images via an electronic image sensor. Digital cameras were developed in the last quarter of the 20th century, from predecessors including video camera tubes. Many compact digital still cameras can record sound and moving video as well as still photographs. Most 21st century cameras are digital.

COMPUTER MICROPHONES

Desktop computer microphones, like the one that might have come with your computer, seem like a good first choice for capturing the sound of your voice. However, in the long run, desktop computer microphones are not a good choice for creating good voice audio, especially recorded messages. There are two main reasons why:

First, desktop computer microphones usually (but not always) contain a multi-directional microphone. This means the pickup sound from all directions. Therefore, in addition to capturing the sound of your voice, they also pick up the sounds from the surroundings.

Second, it is just difficult to record good vocal audio from desktop microphones. Even if the microphone is unidirectional, you have to be close to the actual microphone to minimize background noises.

COMPUTER SPEAKER

Computer speakers help to get the sound output. They range widely in quality and in price. The computer speakers typically packaged with computer systems are small plastic boxes with moderate sound quality. Laptops come with integrated speakers.

MODEMS

Modem is a new word by joining the initial letters of the words modulator and demodulator (***mo****dulator*-***dem****odulator*). It is a device that modulates an analog carrier signal to encode digital information, and also demodulates such a carrier signal to decode the transmitted information. The goal is to produce a signal that can be transmitted easily and decoded to reproduce the original digital data. Modems can be used over networks for transmitting analog signals as well as digital signals.

Modems are generally classified by the amount of data they can send in a given time, normally measured in bits per second (bit/s, or bps). The number of bits a modem can transmit per second is called **bandwidth**. Bandwidth is the unit to measure the transmission speed of communication lines and devices like modem that regulate the transmission. A modem used in coaxial cable for network access is called **cable modem**.

A modem can be considered as an input/output device. Modem is not inputting or outputting data directly, but acts as an intermediary and help input and output.

COMPUTER MEMORY AND PROCESSING HARDWARE

Power supply, motherboard, CPU Chip, Specialized processor chips, RAM Chips, ROM Chips, other forms of memory like cache, VRAM and flash, Expansion slots, boards and various ports constitute processing and memory hardware. Before going into details, let us examine what are processors and its evolution.

Units for measuring computer memory

One should be familiar with the computer memory measurement units

The basic unit of memory measurement is a bit.

A Bit is equivalent to zero '0' or one '1'

8 Bits constitute	1 Byte
1024 Bytes constitute	1 Kilo Byte (1KB) numbers)
1024 Kilobyte:	1 Megabyte (MB)
1024 Megabyte	1 Giga Byte (GB)
1024 Gigabytes	1 Tera Byte (TB)
1024 Terabytes	1 Peta Byte (PB)

(When it is said 1K, it is usually understood as 1000. Actually 1KB is 1022 bytes as computer power is measured by the power of '2'. For convenience it is used to indicate decimal figures. For example, Y2K stands for the year 2000.

PROCESSING AND MEMORY HARDWARE

PROCESSOR

The processor is the computing part or brain of the computer. It is also called the CPU (Central Processing Unit). It is made up of the control unit and ALU. Today, the CPUs of almost all computers are contained on a single chip called microprocessor.

Microprocessor

In early mainframe computers, transistors were used individually and formed electronic circuits with the use of wires and soldering.

Today several transistors are combined to form integrated circuits. That is, a number of transistors are integrated into a single silicon chip. Integrated circuit, microprocessor and microchip are synonymous. In 1961 a chip had only 4 transistors. In 1971 it had 2300, and in 1979 a chip could integrate 30000 transistors. Pentium II, which was released in 1997, had 7.5 million transistors. Pentium III, which was released in 2000, accommodated 40 million transistors and Pentium 4 processor could accommodate more than 65 million and by the turn of the present decade a chip may accommodate 100 million transistors.

MOTHERBOARD

This is also called the "system board". It is the main printed circuit board in an electronic device, which contains sockets that accept additional boards. In a personal computer, the motherboard contains the bus, CPU and coprocessor sockets, memory sockets, keyboard controller and supporting chips.

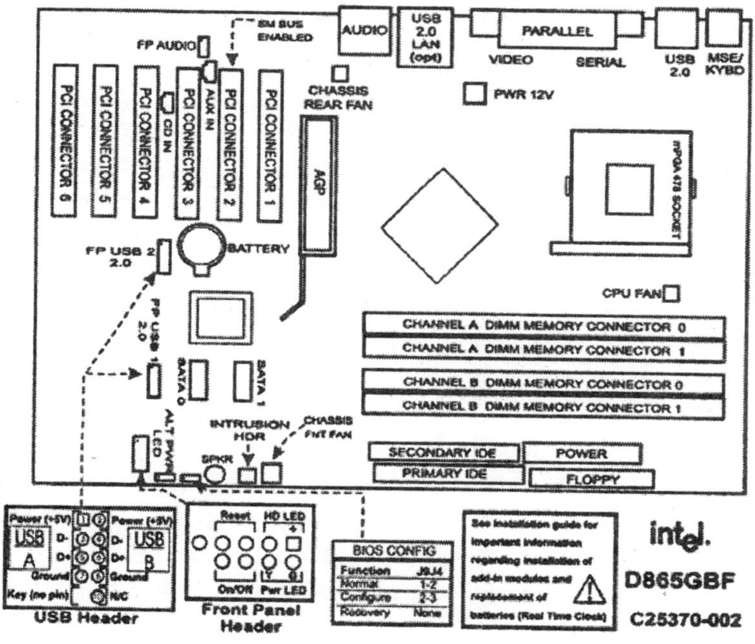

Motherboard

RAM CHIP

When we say computer memory, it refers to the Random Access Memory (RAM). It is also called the primary memory. When we start a computer the memory activated is the RAM. It is the computer's primary workspace. It can consist of one or more memory chips depending on the size of RAM.

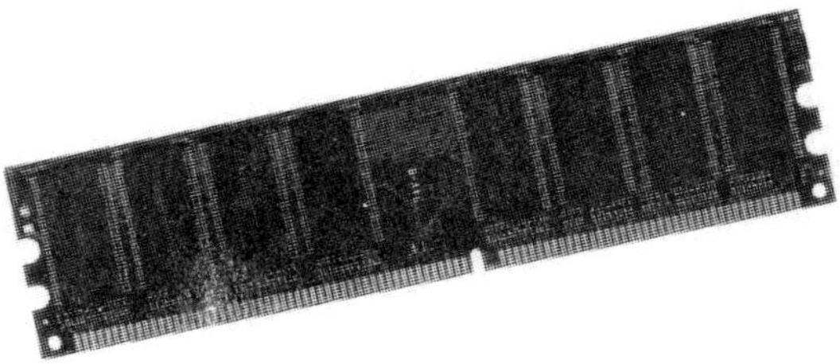

A RAM Chip

STORAGE DEVICES

Hard disk

The most important secondary storage medium, which is made of one or more aluminum or glass platters, coated with a ferromagnetic material. Most hard disks are fixed disks, which are permanently sealed in the drive. Removable hard disks are also available. They can be removed from the computer and used as backup. Hard disks provide fast retrieval because they rotate constantly at high speed, from 5,000 to 15,000 rpm. When personal computers were made during the late 1970s, the hard disk capacity was just 40MB. Now the minimum hard disk capacity for a PC is 500G. The cost of a PC with 40MB hard disk in 1980 was approximately Rs. 80,000.00. Now a PC with 500G hard disk and color display is only Rs. 20,000.00.

Floppy Disks

In personal computers, the common secondary memory device was floppy disks. Even today floppy disk drives are provided in PCs. But floppy disks are no longer used because of low memory size.

Floppy disks were used as movable storage device. When floppies were first used, the size was 8"x8". Next it became 5.25"x5.25" and finally floppies with 3.5"x3.5" became the standard. Now floppies have become obsolete.

When floppy was first used, the size was 8"x8" and independent disk player like a VCR was used. The player was connected to the computer with a cord. In 1977, the disk size was reduced to 5.25"x5.25" and disk drive was made a part of the CPU at the suggestion of Steve Jobs for use in Apple-II computers.Latter disk size was reduced to 3.5"x3.5" with a capacity of 1.2MB The bigger floppies had only a memory capacity of 256K. Now any of these floppies are not used.

Magnetic Tapes

In the days of mainframe computers, during 1960s and 70s, the main secondary storage device used was magnetic tapes. While large spools of tapes were used in mainframe computers, smaller cassette type spools were used in PCs. As random access of data was not possible in tapes, we have to run the tape until the specific information is located. Also it was difficult to preserve tapes for longer time. :Because of these problems, tapes are not used now-a-days.

Optical discs

CD (Compact Disc) : A CD is a digital audio disc that contains up to 74 minutes of hi-fi stereo sound. Introduced in 1982, the disc is a plastic platter 120mm (4.75") in diameter, recorded on one side, with individual selections playable in any sequence. The CDs made for recoding music was called Compact Disc-Digital Audio (CD-DA).

Compact Discs are called optical discs because recording on CDs is done by burning the disc using laser. While reading also laser is used to detect what is recorded on the disc. The spelling 'disk' is used to refer magnetic disks and the spelling 'disc' is used to refer optical discs. Why this distinction is not known.

It was recognized that the CDs used for recording music could be used for recording large quantity of data. The first series of compact discs used for recording information was called CD-ROM (Compact Disc-Read Only Memory). CD-ROMs were used for recording computer software, publications and large computer files. A CD once recorded could not be reused. Initially PCs were provided with CD Drives that could only read from CDs. That is why CDs of those days were called CD-ROM.

Later on PCs were provided with CD readers and writers. Writable and rewritable CDs were produced so that users could write or rewrite on CDs. Such CDs are called CD-W and CD-RW. A CD can accommodate 700 MB of data. CDs provided an ideal secondary storage medium, which could be easily transported.

DVD

Another high density optical storage disc is called DVD (Digital Video/Versatile Disc). DVD is a family of optical discs that are the same as CD in overall dimensions, but have significantly higher capacities. DVDs are also double sided, whereas CDs are single sided. On each side recording can be made in two layers. When recorded on both sides in two layers the total capacity of a DVD can be enhanced up to 17GB.

Pen Drive/Thumb Drive

Pen drive or Flash memory device is a memory chip that can be rewritten and hold its content without power. It is also called a flash memory device as copying to a pen drive can be done very fast without waiting for even a minute. Pen drives are now replacing CDs and DVDs because copying to a pen drive do not require a device like Floppy Drive or DVD Drive. It can be operated from a USB Port. (What is USB Port will be described latter). Recording to and erasing data from the pen drive is very fast. We can have pen drives having 25 GB or more memory. The flash drive was first invented in 1998 by **Dov Moran,** President and CEO of M-Systems Flash Pioneers (Israel).

PORTS

At the back of the CPU of PCs we can find a number of socket for connecting various devices to the computer or network. They are called ports. Port is a pathway into and out of the computer or a network device such as a Modem. For example, the serial and parallel ports on a personal computer are external sockets for plugging in communications lines, modems and printers. Every network adapter has a port for connection to the local area network (LAN). Pen drives are connected to **USB (Universal Serial Bus).**

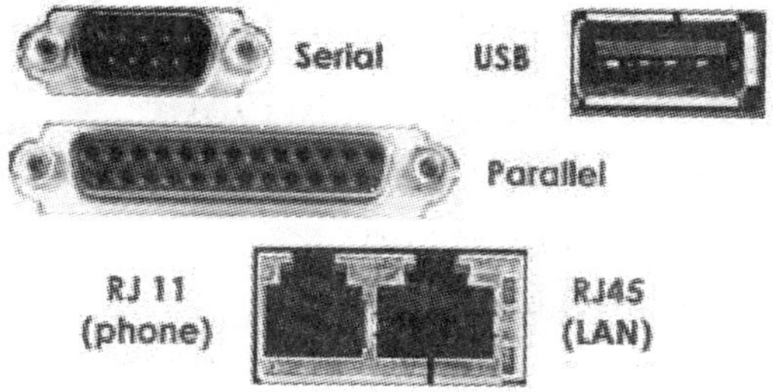

PARALLEL PORT

A parallel port is a type of interface found on computers for connecting peripherals. In computing, a parallel port is a parallel communication physical interface. It is also known as a printer port. Parallel ports have become very uncommon now because you can use USB instead of parallel ports.

SERIAL PORT

A socket on a computer used to connect a modem, mouse, scanner or other serial device via the computer's serial interface is called serial port.

UNIVERSAL SERIAL BUS (USB)

USB (Universal Serial Bus) (pronounced "*YOO-ess-bee*") is a specification to establish communication between devices and a host - usually personal computers. It has become commonplace on other devices such as smart-phones, PDAs and video game consoles, and as a power cord between a device and an AC adapter plugged into a wall plug for charging. USB was invented to make easier connections to external devices to PCs..

COMPUTER LANGUAGE

A computer language or programming language is a set of characters, word and syntactic rules that can be used to write a computer program. Sequential instructions are the stuff of programming language. In fact, one can define a computer program as an exact , step by step set of instructions for completing a specific task. All softwares are written in programming language.

TYPES OF PROGRAMMING LANGUAGE

The major categories of programming languages are:

- Low level languages; and
- High level languages.

Low Level Lanaguage

There are two types of low level languages viz Machine language and Assembly language.

Machine Language

The machine language is the most basic form of programming. Machine code is the most fundamental of programming languages. This is considered as the first generation programming language and is the only one that can be understood by a computer without any translation. The machine code or machine language is a system of instructions and data directly executed by a computer's central processing unit. Machine code is quick in computer operation and makes economical use of computer time. Thus parts of program that are executed frequently are usually written in machine code. This code is the lowest level of abstraction for representing a computer program. Each machine instruction consisted of different permutations of 0s and 1s , and each such instruction could be loaded into the instruction register and executed. A second register , the program counter, was used to keep track of where to go to fetch the next instruction from the main memory.

ASSEMBLY LANGUAGE

The assembly language is slightly more advanced than machine language. The assembly languages simplify the programmer's job by allowing the programmer to use mnemonics in place of '0s' and '1s' in the program. Mnemonics are letters and numbers to represent machine language instructions.

HIGH LEVEL LANGUAGES

The time and cost of creating machine and assembly languages were quite high and this was the prime motivation for the development of high-level languages. Since a high level source program must first translated first into a form the machine can understandand this is done by software called compiler which takes the source code as input and produces as output the machine language code of the machine on which the code is to be executed. During the process of translation the compiler reads the source programs statement-wise and checks the syntactical errors. If there is any error, the compiler generates a print out of the errors it has detected. This action is known as diagnosis. There is another type of software, which does the translation. This is called an interpreter. The compiler and interpreter have different approaches to translation. The high level languages are:

- General purpose language; and
- Specific purpose language

In computer software a general purpse programming language is a language designed to be used for writing software in a wide variety of application domains. In many ways a general purpose language only has this status became it does not include language constructs designed to be used within a specific application domain. The Ada, BASIC, C, C++, COBOL, Fortran, Java, Lisp etc are some of the examples to general programming languages.

Specific purpose language is a computer language specialized to a particular application domain. There are a wide variety of languages such as HTML for web pages. Examples of domain-specific language include HTML, Logo for pencil like drawing, Verilog and VHDL hardware description languages, MATLAB and GNU Octave for matrix programming.

4

SOFTWARE

WHAT IS SOFTWARE?

Software is a set of instructions for the computer. It is also called program. A series of instructions that performs a particular task is called a "program." The two major categories of software are "**system software**" and "**application software.**" System software is also called **operating systems (OS).** Application software is any program that processes data for the user (inventory, payroll, spreadsheet, word processor, etc.). Whether it is operating system or application program, they are created for using a specified set of instructions on the basis of a **computer language**. In this chapter, we will try to understand operating systems or system software, application programs and the languages with which the software packages are created.

OPERATING SYSTEMS OR SYSTEM SOFTWARE

Operating system is the master control program that runs the computer. It is the first program loaded when the computer is turned on. The operating system sets the standards for all application programs that are run in the computer. That is, if you use Windows as the operating system, you can use only application programs compatible with Windows. The **utility programs** and

language translators are also included under the operating software. Utility programs are the programs used for managing a computer. The functions include formatting of disks, partitioning of hard disks, removing viruses, setting password, etc. The applications interact with the operating system for all user interfaces and file management operations. An operating system performs the following functions. An operating system can work without the help of application programs. But application program cannot function without the help of operating systems.

USER INTERFACE

Operating systems help the user to interact with the computer. That is why they are called user interfaces. The common user interfaces are Mac OS, Windows, Linux, etc. These are called graphical user interfaces (GUI), because programs are activated by clicking on the picture representations or Icons. Prior to these GUI systems, all interactions were based on commands entered by the user. Early computers were operated by using machine codes and symbols. In those days operating a computer was not as simple as today. One should be a trained professional to use a computer. Later natural language based operating systems emerged. One such popular operating system was the MS-DOS (Microsoft Disk Operating System) DOS used natural language based verbal instructions to operate a computer. See a few DOS commands.

MD	Make Directory
DR	Display Directory
Del	Delete a file
Dir	Display Directory
Dir/p	Display Directory page by page

DOS was created along with the creation of personal computers. DOS made computer operation very simple and even people without special training could use a computer. Creation of DOS was the first step towards popularization of computer use.

Now we operate the computer using GUI systems, which made computer operation far simpler.

DATA MANAGEMENT

Data management keeps track of the data on disk, tape and optical storage devices. The application program deals with data by file name and a particular location within the file. The operating system's file system knows where that data is physically stored (which sectors on disk) and interaction between the application and operating system is through the programming interface. Whenever an application needs to read or write data, it makes request to the operating system. The operating system loads the file to the application program.

DEVICE MANAGEMENT

Device management controls peripheral devices such as printer, modem, camera, etc., by sending those commands as prescribed by the manufacturer and permitted by the OS. The software that attaches a device to the computer with the help of the OS is known as a "driver.". Thus there are print driver, mouse driver, etc. The operating system contains most of the drivers for the peripherals attached to the computer. When a new peripheral is added, that device's driver is installed into the operating system if it is not already there. When we purchase a peripheral, a CD containing the driver is also supplied along with the peripheral.

SECURITY

Operating systems provide password protection to keep unauthorized users out of the system. Network operating system permits to lock every node with password. Large operating systems also maintain activity logs and accounting of the user's time for billing purposes. Operating Systems allow loading firewall programmes for protecting networks. Operating systems also provide automatic backup and file recovery facilities in the event of a system failure or when electricity is failed.

COMMON OPERATING SYSTEMS

The common operating systems in use are the many versions of Windows (95, 98, NT, ME, 2000, XP, Windows 2008, Windows Vista, Windows 7 and Windows 8), and the many versions of UNIX (Solaris, Linux, etc.), the Macintosh OS, IBM mainframe OS/390 and the AS/400's OS/400. MS-DOS was the first operating system developed at the Microsoft Company to be used with PC. DOS is still used for some legacy applications, and there are other special-purpose operating systems. The following are the functions of operating system:

BOOTING

Booting is the process of causing the computer to start executing instructions. Personal computers contain built-in instructions in a ROM chip that are automatically executed on startup. These instructions search for the operating system, load it and pass control to it. Starting up a large computer may require more button pressing and keyboard input.

The term comes from "bootstrap," since bootstraps help you get your boots on; booting the computer helps it get its first instructions. The term is often used erroneously for application software. You might hear for example, "let's boot Excel," whereas the correct usage is "launch Excel" or "load Excel."

MANAGING STORAGE MEDIA

One of the important functions of the operating system is the administration of any or all of backup, archival, disaster recovery and hierarchical storage management (HSM) procedures. Managing various storage media is another function of the operating system. An example of such a task is formatting of blank diskettes. Before you can use a blank diskette, which you have just bought, you may have to format it. Formatting prepares a diskette to accept data or programs. Nowadays, preformatted disks are available.

PROVIDING USER INTERFACE

The combination of menus, screen design, icons, keyboard commands, commands language and online help, which allows a user to interact with a computer. The input devices other than a keyboard and mouse, like touch pad, and microphone are also considered as user interface. The user interface is the most important part of computer use.

The criteria for the popularity of an operating system are its user friendliness, versatility and affordability. Earlier all computer programmes were functioning on the basis of verbal commands. Later, the commands were given by selecting one item from many options or menu-driven. Towards the late 1980s, clicking the pictorial icons could run most of the software. Such systems , as we have learned, are called graphical user interfaces (gui). Voice recognition user interfaces will be the next dimension. "What you say is what you get" (WYSIWYG).

FILE MANAGEMENT

It refers to the activity of managing files on a disk. It provides functions to delete, copy, move, rename, back up and view files as well as create and manage directories. The file manager in Windows 3.1 it was appropriately named File Manager. In later editions of Windows the file manager is known as Windows Explorer. The file managers provide the ability to create, enter, change, query and produce reports on one file at a time.

TASK MANAGEMENT

Multitasking, which is the ability to simultaneously execute multiple programs, is available in all operating systems today. In the desktop world, multitasking is necessary just for keeping several applications open at the same time so you can bounce back and forth between them.

WINDOWS

Windows is the most widely used operating system for personal computers. Windows provides a graphical user interface and desktop environment similar to the Macintosh, in which applications are displayed in re-sizable, movable windows on screen.

Windows contains built-in networking, which allows users to share files and applications if more than one PCs, which are connected to a network. The server versions of Windows are Windows NT and Windows 2000. All latest versions of Windows support networks.

ADVANTAGES OF WINDOWS

The single advantage to Windows is the huge wealth of application programs that have been written for it. It is the de facto standard for desktop and laptop computers worldwide with hundreds of millions of users. In many cases, people no longer ask what platform software runs on. If you use a computer, they expect it to be Windows. Windows is supported by Microsoft, the largest software company in the world.

DISADVANTAGES OF WINDOWS

Issuing new versions at shorter intervals is a disadvantage. By the time a user learns about the version installed in his or her computer a new version is released. From the point of view of software business, frequent change may be good. From the point of view of user, frequent updating may be better. Compared to Windows, the Mac has always been more consistent and easier to use than Windows. But the disadvantage of the Mac is that there are fewer Mac applications on the market than for Windows. A number of versions of Windows appeared in the market since 1995. They are presented in the following table:

WHAT'S A WINDOW?

A window is a rectangular area on screen surrounded by a window frame with a title bar and title at the top. Each time you launch (run) a Windows application, it is displayed in its own window, and you can launch additional applications and work with all of them.

If your screen is big enough, you can place windows side by side or overlap them so you can see more than one document at the same time. You can move windows around, make them smaller or let them take up the full screen and easily switch between them.

Windows Version	Year of release	Main features
Windows 1.0	1985	The original version of Microsoft Windows introduced in late 1985. It provided a graphical interface under DOS. It displayed tiled windows (side by side) and was never popular.
Windows 2.0	1987	An upgrade to Windows 1.0, it was later renamed Windows/286.
Windows 3.0	1990	It was widely supported because of its improved interface and ability to manage large amounts of memory.
Windows 3.1	1992	A major upgrade to Windows 3.0. It added support for multimedia. Windows 3.1 ran 16-bit Windows and DOS applications.
Windows 3.11	1993	An upgrade to and the final release of Windows 3.1.
Windows95	1995	Windows 95 is a 32-bit operating system designed to replace the 16-bit Windows 3.1.
Windows 98	June 1998	A major upgrade to Windows 95. Removed

		bugs and improved performance. Supports more hardware, including the USB.
Windows 98 SE	Sept. 1998	An upgrade to Windows 98. It incorporates Windows 98 Service Pack 1 with Internet Explorer 5, Outlook Express 5, NetMeeting 3 and Media Player 6.1. bundled.
Windows ME (Windows Millennium Edition)	May 2000	An upgrade to Windows 98 Windows ME adds more support for digital cameras, multi-player games on the Internet and home networking.
Windows NT (Windows New Technology)	2000	A 32-bit operating system for PC networking.
Windows 2000	Feb. 2000	Also known as "Win2K" and "W2K," it is a major upgrade to Windows NT 4. *See detailed description*
Windows XP	2001	An upgraded client version of Windows 2000. Introduced in 2001
Windows 2003	2003	A thoroughly revised edition of Windows 2000Server
Windows Vista	2007	A thoroughly revised version of Windows XP
Windows 2008	2008	Most of the functions can be selected from menu. A very improved version of 2003
Windows 7	2009	Created for home and business desktops, laptops, netbooks, tablet PCs, and media center PCs.
Windows 8	2012	In addition to features of Windows 7, it improved user experience on mobile devices such as tablets and mobile devices which uses other mobile operating systems like Android and Apple's iOS.

LINUX

Linux is version of UNIX that runs on a variety of hardware platforms including PCs. Linux is open source software, which is freely available; however, the full distribution of Linux along with technical support and training are available for a fee from vendors such as **Red Hat Software** (www.redhat.com) and **Caldera** (www.caldera.com). The CD-ROMs in which the software is distributed contain the complete source code. If you want, you can modify the program to suit your requirement. That is why; the source code is also included.

In 1990, Finnish computer science student Linus Torvalds converted **Minix**, a popular classroom-teaching tool, into **Linux**, which is closer to the real UNIX. Torvalds created the kernel, and most of the supporting applications and utilities came from the **GNU project** of the Free Software Foundation. Many programmers have contributed to the **Linux/GNU** system. VA Linux Systems provides a Web site devoted entirely to Linux **(www.linux.com).**

FREE SOFTWARE

Free software is software that can be used, studied, and modified without restriction, and which can be copied and redistributed in modified or unmodified form either without restriction, or with minimal restrictions. Free software is generally available without charge, but occasionally a fee can be charged for installation or to support free software movement.

In practice, for software to be distributed as free software, the human-readable form of the program (the source code) must be made available to the recipient along with a notice granting the above permissions. Such a notice is either a "free software license", or a notice that the source code is released into the public domain.

FREE SOFTWARE MOVEMENT

The free software movement was conceived in 1983 by Richard Stallman to enjoy "software freedom" by computer users. Stallman founded the Free Software Foundation in 1985 to provide the organizational structure to advance his Free Software ideas. From 1998 onwards, alternative terms for free software came into use. The most common are "software libre", "free and open source software" ("FOSS") and "free, libre and open source software" ("FLOSS"). The "Software Freedom Law Center" was founded in 2005 to protect and advance FLOSS. The opposite of free software is "**proprietary software**" or "**non-free software**". Commercial software may be either free software or proprietary software, contrary to a popular misconception that "commercial software" is a synonym for "proprietary software". (An example of commercial free software is Red Hat Linux.)

NETWORK OPERATING SYSTEMS

NOVELL

In 1983 Novell, Inc., concentrated on the development of its NetWare operating system. In the early 1990s, NetWare became the most widely used server operating system for PC networks. It planned to integrate UnixWare and NetWare into a "super" network operating system. During the 1990s NetWare became the main network operating systems from Novell that support DOS, Windows, OS/2 and Macintosh clients. In the early 1990s, NetWare was the largest LAN operating systems installed. TCP/IP (Transmission Control Protocol/Internet Protocol) is the network software used in the Internet. The name Internet is given to the global network of networks thanks to TCP/IP. It is an internetworking software as it connects all types of networks and individual computers. It was introduced in 1883.

UNIX

Ken Thompson at AT&T developed UNIX in 1969. More work was done by Dennis Ritchie, and, by 1974, UNIX had matured into an efficient operating system. UNIX became very popular in scientific and academic environments. Considerable enhancements were made to UNIX at the University of California at Berkeley, and versions of UNIX with the Berkeley extensions became widely used. By the late 1970s, commercial versions of UNIX, became available.

UTILITY PROGRAMS

A program is that supports the proper use of computer. Utility programs, or "utilities," that support everyday uses of the computer include file management (creating, moving and renaming folders, copying and deleting files), searching for files, comparing file contents as well as performing diagnostic routines to check performance and current health of the hardware. Utility programs can include file recovery programs and programs like Norton anti-virus programs also. The principal services provided by the utility programs are:

- **Create backup :** of files and programs.
- **Make data recovery :** when the computer breaks down or when files are accidentally deleted.
- **File defragmentation :** for setting fragmented files into proper order.
- **Disk repair :** which involves checking the disks for defects and repairs on the spot or mark the bad sectors.
- **Virus protection :** Using antivirus software the disks are scanned and the viruses are either removed or made inactive.
- **Data Compression :** Encoding data to take up less storage space. Special utiltities are used for data compression. WinZip is one such utility. There are two types of data compression – **lossless compression** and **lossy compression.** When text and financial data are compressed, they must be decompressed back to a perfect original. This is known as "lossless compression." However, audio and video can be compressed to as little as 5% of its original size using "lossy compression." Some of the data is actually lost, but the loss is not noticeable to the human ear and eye.
- **Memory Management :** Refers to a variety of methods used to store data and programs in

memory, keep track of them and reclaim the memory space when they are no longer needed.

APPLICATION SOFTWARE

Application software as the name indicates software packages used for various tasks that we perform using computers. Thus we have software for entertainment, learning carrying out tasks like word processing, accounting, database management, etc.

We have made a very general survey of system software. Let us see what are application software and what are the different types of application software. Broadly there are five categories of application software. They are:

1. Entertainment software
2. Home or personal software
3. Education or Reference Software
4. Productivity software
5. Specialty software

Let us consider each of these categories.

ENTERTAINMENT SOFTWARE

Video games might seem silly, but they are more important than you might think. There are packages that permit you to use in a PC or in a network environment. There are number of cites in the Internet providing only games. Atomic Bomberman, Pong, Space Invaders, Pac-Man, Super Mario, Hedgehog, Mortal Combat, etc. are some of the popular computer games. It is said that children who play computer games may help children learn better and they think differently from others who are not playing computer games. The sales of computer games in the United States alone could generate an annual income of $3.5 billion Dollar.

HOME OR PERSONAL SOFTWARE

Home or personal software include, software for cookery, home management, gardening, travel planning etc. Graham Kerr's Swiftly Seasoned is a CD ROM containing recipes for 140 exotic food items. Jenny Craig Cookbook and Completely Interactive Cookbook are two other examples. There are number of tourist guides with maps and details about places of attraction and hotels are available in the CD format and online.

EDUCATIONAL AND REFERENCE SOFTWARE

CBT (Computer-Based Training) is the method of using the computer for training and instruction. CBT programs are called "courseware" and provide interactive training sessions for all disciplines. There are also software packages specializing in self-study courses that users can take at their own PCs, CBT programs are available in plenty from the net. If you are interested you can learn any computer program by downloading tutorials.

PRODUCTIVITY SOFTWARE

This is a very important category and majority of the programs come under this category. The programs that come under this category can be further grouped into the following sub categories:

- Word processing software
- Spreadsheet software
- Database management software including personal information managers and library automation packages
- Financial Software including personal finance programs
- Software for cyberspace – Communication protocols, web browsers, news groups, etc.
- Content access software

- Simulation software
- Integrated Software suites

WORD PROCESSING

This involves the creation of text documents. Advanced word processors function as elementary desktop publishing systems. Although there are still machines dedicated only to word processing, most word processing is performed on general-purpose computers using word processing software such as Microsoft Word and WordPerfect.

According to another classification, application software packages comes under two broad categories – horizontal applications and vertical applications

1. **Horizontal applications** are general purpose applications such as word processing, slide presentation, database management, etc. Most of the application programs belong to this category.
2. **Vertical Applications** are software packages designed to perform a specific function in specialized institutions. For example, software developed for running super markets, Software developed for banking, etc. come under this category. This kind of software packages are developed usually on the basis of specific requirements of organizations. Thus we have application software for horizontal applications and vertical applications.

SOFTWARE SUITE

INTEGRATED SOFTWARE SUITES

This includes software that combines several applications in one program, typically database management, word processing, spreadsheet, business graphics and communications. Such programs Microsoft Office, Star Office, etc. are examples for integrated software suite. Integrated software suits are created to put related programs at one place. In Microsoft Office the following are the important programs included:

MS-Word

MS-Excel

MS-PowerPoint

MS-Access

MS-Publisher

5

LIBRARY AUTOMATION

INTRODUCTION

Automation is a process of using the machineries for easily working and saving manpower and time. The main objective of library automation is to free the librarians and library staff and to allow them to contribute more meaningfully to disseminate knowledge and information. In fact when we use machineries for collection, processing, storage and retrieval of information and do other types of works of library with the help of machineries is called library automation.

The computerisation is the part of library automation. The use of computer technology for library housekeeping operations and information storage and retrieval is known as library computerisation.

HISTORY

The history of library computerisation can be divided into three phases viz i)Experimental system phase ii) Local system phase and ; iii) Cooperative system phase.

i) Experimental system phase

In the early 1960s several libraries in developed countries like the USA and the UK began to experiment with using computers to assist in the processing of information . Several of these systems evolved from punched-card data processing system. Some of the computer systems developed during this phase failed due to inadequate computer technology, lack of understanding between librarians and computer specialists.

ii) Local System Phase

The late 1960s is considered as the local system phase. Many librarians made use of computers as a tool in the organisation of the library activities. Most of these computer systems developed locally either in academic library, special library or in public library. This phase of computerisation was success due the reasons that the computer technology was improved and better understanding was made between librarians and computer specialists.

iii) Co-operative System Phase

During 1970s libraries started cooperation and resource sharing by computer based systems. Cooperative systems like BLCMP(Birmingham Libraries Cooperative Mechanisation Project) in the UK and OCLC (Online Computer Library Centre) in the USA are striking examples to library cooperation and resource sharing during this phase.

During from the 1960s the first use of library automation was the use of computers to store bibliographic data and to enable the circulation of stock. The project to place onto computer the stock of the US Library of Congress resulted ultimately in the development of machine-readable cataloguing(MARC), opening up the possibility of libraries exchanging bibliographic records and encouraging cooperation between libraries. In the 1970s the library management system became the main housekeeping tool in large libraries and this trend was continued through the following two decades, leaving very few libraries without some form of system. Other fundamental developments began to bring about the convergence of the hitherto specialised library automation environment with the developments underway in the larger computer industry . These were the increasing power in the performance of the personal computer ; the increasing predominance of non-proprietary software, encouraging competition but just as importantly enabling increasing exchange of data over networks; and the development of the Internet.

In India many attempts were made on computerisation of library and information activities in the form of seminars, conferences and workshops and short term courses organised by various organisations. Most of these were sponsored by the Department of Science and Industrial Research(DSIR) and University Gants Commission)UGC). Attempts made by Indian National Documentation Centre(INSDOC) New Delhi(now NISCAIR), Documentation Research Centre(DRTC), Bangalore, National Aeronautical Laboratory(NAL) Bangalore in the area of library computerisation are remarkable.

NEED FOR LIBRARY AUTOMATION

The following factors necessitated the need for library automation

- Information explosion
- Availability of information sources in various formats such as print, non-print, graphical, audio-visual etc
- Different approaches and needs of user community
- Limitation of the library such as time, space and manpower
- Duplication of house keeping operations
- Develop good management of information retrieval system
- To obtain increased operational efficiencies

- To search national and international databases
- Impact of information communication technology
- To improve the quality ,speed and effectiveness of services
- To improve access the resources on other networks and systems, including the websites
- Enable the libraries to participate in resources sharing
- To improve the management of their physical and financial resources
- To facilitate wider dissemination of the information products and services

OBJECTIVES OF LIBRARY AUTOMATION

The objectives of library automation are;

1. Speedy disposal of library work
2. Establishment of a well storage and retrieval system
3. Time and manpower saving with qualitative services
4. Simplicity in library management to meet the objectives
5. Suitability of library cooperation and coordination development
6. Development of manpower resources
7. Proper use of manpower resources
8. Development of new and improved services
9. Preparation of reports and correspondence
10. Suitability for resource sharing and networking.

ADVANTAGES OF LIBRARY AUTOMATION

The advantages are:

- Easily search information
- Time saving
- Speedy communication

- Helpful in stock verification
- Easily working with the help of automation
- Helpful in resource sharing
- It motivate to library staff
- Development of manpower resource

BASIC REQUIREMENTS FOR LIBRARY AUTOMATION

The basic requirements for library automation are:

- Adequate collection
- Adequate finance
- Hardware
- Software
- Trained staff
- User training
- Maintenance and development.

APPLICATION OF COMPUTERS IN LIBRARY AND INFORMATION FIELD

Computers are used in libraries to assist in the areas:

i) House keeping operations and ii) Information storage and retrieval

HOUSE KEEPING OPERATIONS

The house keeping procedures in a library are those which are necessary for the administration of the library. These can be categorised as the following

- Acquisition
- Cataloguing
- Circulation
- Serials Control
- Stock verification
- Administration and Maintenance

a) Acquisition

The acquisition system constitutes selection, ordering and accessioning of documents into the library's collection. The activities or functions of the acquisition system are the following:

- **Selection :** This constitutes the activities such as duplication checking and completion of bibliographic data of the document
- **Ordering :** The activities involved in this step are : Discount patterns, vendor assignment, order placement, status of receipt of the book, notices for claims and cancellation of orders, if necessary.
- **Accessioning :** The activities of this step are : Matching of the received items with orders given, budget control, payment status etc

To maintain and run the acquisition system the following files shall be required.

i) **Holding file :** This file denotes the file relating to the existing collection of the library

ii) **Order file :** Order number, bibliographical details, main listing of books , budget etc

iii) **Supplier file :** It records the detailed information of the books listing and other bibliographical details of the needed publications by the users

iv) **Fund file :** It keeps the subject-wise allocated amount of library budget

v) **Currency file :** It keeps the record of the details of the book and accession number.

b) Cataloguing

It is the list of the book made available for use by given author, title, subject and other approaches. The main objective is to provide the information of availability of books in the library to the user.

The following files are to be maintained.

i) **Master file :** It is made after making few additions and alterations in book receipt

ii) **Index file :** This file contains the different entries like author, heading and subject as an information

iii) **Authority file :** Publisher, institution, language etc are entered in the file for information retrieval .

c) Classification

Classification by the computer has its own limitations. Therefore appropriate class number is decided for a particular book and the number is entered by the computer . Separate programmes are made for different classification schemes.

d) Circulation

Circulation control is the most important function of a library. This work can be done with efficiently and speedily. The circulation work includes the following activities:

i) To issue and return of books

ii) To reserve books

iii) To provide the information for a book needed by the user

iv) To renew the date of issued book if required by the user

v) To calculate the fine for overdue books

vi) To prepare reminder for users in respect of over due books

vii) To prepare issue statistics.

e) Serials Control

The periodicals or serials do not have any specific periodicity and have many issues like the change of frequency, change of name, non-receipt of issues etc. All these issues are handled by the serial control module of the software. The serial control includes the following activities

i) To make input entry of serial data

ii) To maintain record of newly subscribed periodicals and its receipt record

iii) To get knowledge whether the up-to-date record is maintained for incoming periodicals

iv) To make the list of the missing serial

v) To send remainder to the vendor for non-receipt of periodicals

vi) To maintain the record of payment

vii) To make updating of periodical list.

f) Stock verification

In earlier days, stock verification was a cumbersome job in libraries. Now computer is used very effectively for stock verification. Accession number from beginning number to last is entered as input of computer. Then the numbered book available in the library stock including issued books, books in the technical section for processing, interlibrary loan books and books send for binding are entered in the computer. The total accession number is tallied with the books available and a list of non available books (missing books) is prepared

g) Administration and Maintenance

With the application of computers in libraries a number of administrative activities can be carried out very effectively and efficiently. The administrative activities include :

i) To prepare the reports of the meetings

ii) To make copies of library rules

iii) To make record of leave of library staff

iv) To maintain filing of registers and administrative orders

v) To maintain salary and other service details of library staff

INFORMATION STORAGE AND RETRIEVAL

The computerised information storage and retrieval system provides quite a good number of value added information services by using information content . Automated information retrieval systems provide retrospective and current information searches to the users very effectively and efficiently. The computer-based information services are given below.

ON-LINE PUBLIC ACCESS CATALOGUE (OPAC)

The computerised on-line catalogue is popularly known as On-line Public Access Catalogue(OPAC). It is computerised database of library holdings. OPAC can be searched locally and on-line through internet. Information search is possible by using the name of author, title, subject key terms of the book. Information search is possible by combining key terms by using Boolean logical operators like AND, OR and NOT. OPAC helps to understand the current status of a book, whether it is loaned out or available on the shelf?. An internet enabled OPAC is known as Web OPAC.

BIBLIOGRAPHICAL SERVICES

Quite a good number of bibliographical services can be rendered to the user community by generating bibliographies on their subject of interest. Information services like indexing and abstracting services are also fall under bibliographical services.

REFERENCE SERVICE

The concept of reference service is the process of establishing contact between reader and his documents in a personal way. Computers are used very effectively for effective efficient reference service Today a number of reference access tools are available through offline data bases available in CD ROMs and on-line data bases available through internet. If the reference service is provided through on-line it is called on-line reference service or digital reference service or virtual reference service.

CURRENT AWARENESS SERVICES(CAS)

Current awareness service connotes being well informed over wide areas going beyond the fields which are obviously and directly relevant to current activities. Harrod's Librarians' Glossary defines current awareness service as 'a system, and often a publication, for notifying current documents to users of libraries and information services'.

Current awareness services are devices meant for speedy announcement of newly acquired information or documents. Timeliness is the essence of this service, and it is therefore also called as an alerting mechanism. The main objective of this service is to keep the research, development and management personal of the organisation and other interested organisations abreast of the current developments in their respective fields of specialisation as quickly as possible.

TYPES OF CURRENT AWARENESS SERVICES

The current awareness services can be broadly categorised into two types. They are:

- Those services which are directed towards all users; and
- Those services which are directed towards individuals or group of users.

There are various types of current awareness services which can be directed towards all types of users without any discrimination of their areas of interest .They are:

Addition List or Accession List

This is the list of latest additions or accessioned document. Compiled in a library. This list is usually brought out as a current awareness tool presuming the fact that the list contains latest publications in various subject areas acquired by a library.

Contents pages of Journals

This service is based on the contents pages of journals received in a library. The computer generated contents pages can be systematically arranged alphabetically on the basis of the title of the journal and then circulated to users.

News Paper Clipping Service

Important information pertaining to certain subject areas that are of institutional interest may be published in the news papers. Such information may be scanned and important items may be cut from the news papers and brought the same under the notice of the users.

Library Bulletin

Library bulletin may be in the form of news bulletin generated from libraries giving items of current general information such as addition list, list of contents of journals, indexes and abstracts, research studies completed, research in progress etc.

Routing of periodicals

It is an important means of dissemination of current information. There are two types of routing that can be followed such as radial routing and circular routing.

SELECTIVE DISSEMINATION OF INFORMATION (SDI)

Selective Dissemination of Information (SDI) is based on the concept of intensified personal service. It is one of those services which are directed towards individuals so as to cater to individual requirements. It is a refinement of current awareness service. This concept was conceived by H.P.Luhn in 1961.

A computerised SDI system comprises the following steps.

- Construction of users' profile
- Construction of document profile
- Matching mechanism
- Issue of notification
- Feedback from users
- Modification of the users' profile, if needed.

CONSTRUCTION OF USERS' PROFILE

This step consists of creating profile of the users who are to be given SDI service. A profile consists of name of the user, address, status, key words relating to the subject specialisation of the user etc. The collected user profiles should form an input in the computer

CONSTRUCTION OF DOCUMENT PROFILE

This step involves the construction of database of the documents. Each document received by the library is scanned, indexed and abstracted. Proper subject analysis of the document is extremely important for the success of the SDI service. The document profile contains, name of the author,, title of the document, key words represents the subject of the article etc. The document profiles form another input in the computer system.

MATCHING MECHANISM

In the matching mechanism, at a pre-determined stage the computer match two inputs viz users' profile and document profiles by a programme. This matching process produces output as notification.

ISSUE OF NOTIFICATION

The output is printed by the system in the form of two cards. One card is known as 'information card' which contains details about documents or information itself matched for the specific user by the system. Another card is known as 'response card' which contains information to be furnished by the user and return to the library as a feedback mechanism to ascertain the degree of usefulness of information retrieved.

PROFILE MODIFICATION

In the process of going through the notifications, a user may indicate the usefulness of the documents disseminated to him/her or point out that output provided in the information card was relevant or partially relevant or not at all relevant. At this stage , the SDI system is to modify the particular profile in case the user opines that the information was not relevant or partially relevant. This implies that modification of the users' profile is guided largely by the feedback provided by the user.

6

LIBRARY MANAGEMENT SOFTWARE

A software is a set of programmes written or developed to enable the computer to do desired operations. The software can be broadly categorised into two types :

- System software ; and
- Application software

The system software is otherwise known as operating system. Which is set of programmes inbuilt in computers to run the computer whereas application software is used in the computer to perform specific applications. In the case of libraries, application software is used to automate house keeping operations and information storage and retrieval purposes.

The software are also categorised , based on their functions such as :

i) Basic software for data entry, validation etc;

ii) Word processing software to manipulate text-storage;

iii) Database management systems(DBMS) for management of databases;

iv) Text-retrieval packages for storage and retrieval of non-numeric records;

v) Software associated with searching on-line retrieval system and CDROM databases; and

vi) Library house keeping software.

LIBRARY MANAGEMENT SOFTWARE

There are quite a good number of library software packages available. CDS/ISIS, ALICE for Windows, Minisis The Library Program,Sanjay, LIBSYS, Maitreyi, Wylisys, DELMS, ILMS, ARCHIVES, LIBMAN, LIBSOFT, LIBRA, LIBRARIAN, LIBRIS, MEMLIB Krvger Library Manager, Trishna, Ulysis SOUL, PALMS ODYSSEY etc are some of the software packages used as library management software in libraries . Brief description about some of the important library software is given below.

CDS/ISIS

The acronym CDS/ISIS stands for Computerised Documentation System/ Integrated Set of Information System. CDS/ISIS has been designed and developed by UNESCO's Division of Software Development Applications Office of Information Programmes and Services. It is a menu-driven generalised information storage and retrieval system, designed specifically for computerised management of databases. The software is highly useful and fast in creating bibliographic databases for information storage and retrieval. But the menus provided in the software are not adequate for library house keeping operations. Nevertheless, the software allows creation of additional menus for such operations through writing programmes in Pascal language. The important features of this package are:

i) the package allows its users to create non-numerical databases;

ii) the database can accommodate over one crore sixty lakh records;

iii) the maximum size of display format is of 4,000 characters;

iv) there are menus and sub menus which provide options;

v) it allows the use to enter new records in a database and edit, modify ,delete, print, display or browse the existing records;

vi) it allows the user to create database/s on his/her own;

vii) the status information is displayed as soon as a database is selected;

viii) its indexing capabilities are extremely dependable and fast;

ix) its search facilities are simple, accurate and rapid;

x) details of search results can be seen immediately on VDU and also can be printed /copied;

xi) it allows the users to make their own menus and sub menus and their own programmes through advance programming.

LIBSYS

This package is developed by Libsys corporation, New Delhi. It is fully integrated multi-user library system designed to run on a wide spectrum of hardware/software platforms in client-server environment. It is easy to operate and the library staff can begin to use it quickly without much computer skills. It ensures high productivity because of minimal data entry requirements, maximum possible integration of functions and powerful search and query facilities. It has its own centralised bibliographic database based on ANSI Z39.50 format. LIBSYS supports almost all activities relating to acquisition, cataloguing, circulation and serials control and has a powerful but at the same time user friendly OPAC interface.

LIBSYS is highly user-friendly having features such as integrated functions, interactive and screen oriented, menu driven, multi user capabilities, minimum possible data entry, powerful data editing facility, easily installable, user defined security, database recovery procedure, help facility etc. It is well proved software having quite a good number of registered users in Asian countries. The registered users include university libraries, public libraries, Governmental organisations, British libraries etc.

SOUL

The SOUL(Software for University Libraries) is a library software package developed by INFLIBNET centre, an IUC of University Grants Commission, Ahmedabad as a total solution for library automation and management. The SOUL is designed using client server architecture which imparts extra strength to storage capacity, and has multiple access to single database, various levels of security , backup storage facilities etc. This software was designed after a comprehensive study of different library related functions practiced in university libraries. It has MS-SQL server 6.5 RDMS as the back end. This user friendly software is quite easy to work. It contains modules viz Acquisition, Catalogue, Circulation, Serial Control, Administration and OPAC

The in-built network features of the software will allow multiple libraries of the universities to function together and access to distributed databases installed at various university libraries and union catalogue mounted at INFLIBNET using VSAT network

The acquisition module enables library staff to handle the following major functions of library materials viz i) Suggestion management; ii) ordering; iii)cancellation and reminders iv) receiving; v)payment including fund control; and master file management such as currency table, vendors, publisher, user etc.

The catalogue module is used for retrospective conversion of books, technical processing of books received from acquisition section, printing of records for verification, searching by title and accession numbers, the authority files for publishers etc. One of the unique features of SOUL is its access to authority files on screen as well as selection box in various fields of records. Once the proposed VSAT Network by INFLIBNWT is commissioned, this module will take care of automatic replication of data into union catalogue. This will avoid exchange of library data on physical media i.e floppy, tape etc. This module covers the functions such as catalogue process, catalogue search, user services, catalogue card generation, authority file maintenance, retro conversion, stock verification report generation, union database maintenance ; and export of records.

The circulation module will take care of all possible functions dealt in a university library set up. Starting from membership management , maintenance of status of library items can be handled using SOUL. The circulation transactions viz issue, return, renewal, reserve, recall, hold can be done successfully . The complex functions like fine management for each category of user and material can also be effectively carried out . Inter library loan, searching the status of every member or library item are also possible. Reminders of overdue material, generation of various reports have also been covered.

The On-line Public Access Catalogue(OPAC) of SOUL is a window to the library collection. Using the user friendly menu , user can search for an item available in the library by author , title, corporate author, conference name, subject descriptor , class number etc. The Boolean search enables the user to conduct the search using all combinations including type of materials, language, year etc. Besides, this will serve as first point of information about the library and also gateway for accessing

INTERNET union database or any other external sources.

The complex job of keeping serials control is effectively handled by serial control module. This module handles the functions such as suggestions, subscription, payment including fund control, check of uses, issue arrival, reminder generation, binding management, search status of every item, master database management, report generation etc.

User administration module is used for creating new users and giving them right for accessing different modules

The SOUL is a suitable package to work under university environment. Moreover, the network features of the software will allow multiple libraries of university to function together.

OPEN LIBRARY SOFTWARE

Evergreen, Koha, NewGenLib, OpenBiblio, PMB etc are some of the examples to integrated library system. These are free library software packages which can be used, studied and modified without restriction or with minimum restriction.

EVALUATION OF LIBRARY SOFTWARE

Today, quite a good number of library software packages developed in foreign countries and India available to librarians for library automation. The question before librarian is which library software package should be purchased out of the large number of packages that are available through commercial channel? What are the criteria or checklist to be considered in the selection of software package? Computerisation of a library requires a lot of money, manpower and materials. The computerised library system may affect positively or negatively the efficiency of a library because of the particular software package used by the library . Hence an objective assessment or evaluation of the packages is required in the choice of particular software for automation. The criteria for the selection of software are the following.

i) Locate and evaluate a knowledgeable dealer or sales person.

ii) Thoroughly examine the documentation of the software you are considering

iii) Arrange for a demonstration of the software

iv) Prepare yourself before the demonstration

v) Put the programme through its paces

vi) Evaluate the quality of the after sales support you can expect from the dealer or vendor.

In general, the selection or choice of anything is a difficult job. In the case of software selection, each software has its own merits and demerits. It is the duty of the librarian to assess the positive and negative aspects of the software package and select the appropriate one which is suitable for the library. In fact, the selection of the software, aspects such as the objective of the library, collection, services to be generated from the library, user-friendly nature of the software, cost, compatibility, authoritativeness of the firm which desired the software, after sales service support etc should be considered.

7

COMPUTER NETWORKS

The concept of library networking has gained wide popularity with the application of computers in libraries. A network is a physically separate computers with telecommunication links through which they can exchange information and share resources. Also used in the abstract sense to mean modes of interaction between people . By computer network is meant interconnected and interlinked computer systems. In other words, it is a system in which many computer points and terminals stretching over a room or building or city, or State or nation or the world are connected with each other for information communication. Thus ,the term library network refers to interlinked libraries.

NEED FOR LIBRARY NETWORKING

Library networking ensures high degree of resource sharing among libraries and information centres. It was in 1984 that a Working Group of Planning Commission emphasised in their report to the Government of India for interlinking of library services by modernising libraries and information centres. This paved the way for computerised networking among libraries in India. The need and utility of networked system are the following.

To ensure economy

It is a common experience that at one hand the financial resources of libraries are shrinking and on other hand the cost escalation of books and periodicals. In such a situation it is expected from libraries to enter into resource sharing through computerised networking. Each library can have the benefit of searching resources of other libraries participating in the network. Computerised library networking is therefore required for ensuring economic factor.

To encounter the pressure of information explosion

The exponential growth of literature paved the way for information explosion. In this context no library how big it may be think of becoming self sufficient . In order to encounter the pressure created by information explosion , it is essential to develop computerised networking among libraries and information centres.

TYPES OF LIBRARY NETWORKS

Library networks are categorised on the basis of the area covered as follows:

LAN

LAN Stands for Local Area Network. It is a network covering a small geographic area, like a building or office. This is known as LAN because all the terminals and peripherals linked by cabling to the central processor kept at the work station. A LAN has two major components viz hardware and software. The hardware consists of workstation, cables, server, repeaters, hub,bridge and gateway. Library network in the Kerala university library, Net work in the Trivandrum public library etc are examples to LAN

WAN

WAN stands for Wide Area Network. WAN is a network system which operates in a wider area stretching across a city, State, region, nation or the world. WAN is used to connect LANs and other types of networks together, so that users and computers in one location can communicate with users and computers in other locations. Information and Library Network(INFLIBNET), Internet etc are examples to WAN

MAN

MAN stands for Metropolitan Area network. It is a network covering the geographical area city. Ahmedabad Library Network (ADINET), Bangalore Library Network, Bombay Library Network, Calcutta Library Network (CALIBNET) Developing Library Network (DELNET), Madras Library Network(MALIBNET) Mysore Library Network(MYLIBNET), Pune Library Network etc are some of the important Metropolitan area networks in India.

CAN

CAN stands for Campus Area Network. It is a network covering the buildings in a campus area . Kerala university campus area network, Madras IIT campus area network etc are examples to CAN

TOPOLOGY

Topology is meant the network's blue print or mapping of the network. It is the way in which different units(computers) within the network are connected with each other. The various types of topology are the following

Star Network

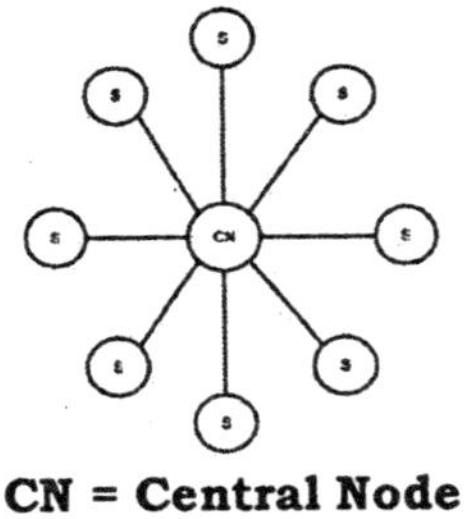

CN = Central Node

S = Subscriber Node

It consists of one central node and a number of other subscriber terminals connected to the central point using single line for each connection.

Bus Network

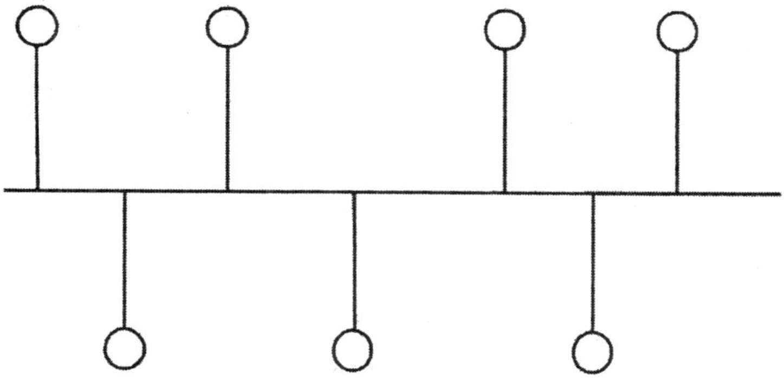

It consists of number of nodes linked to a 'Central Communication Highway' or 'bus' in such a way that every node has a single bi-directional connection to a shared cable which enables each node to be directly connected to each of the rest of the nodes over this shared cable.

Mesh Network

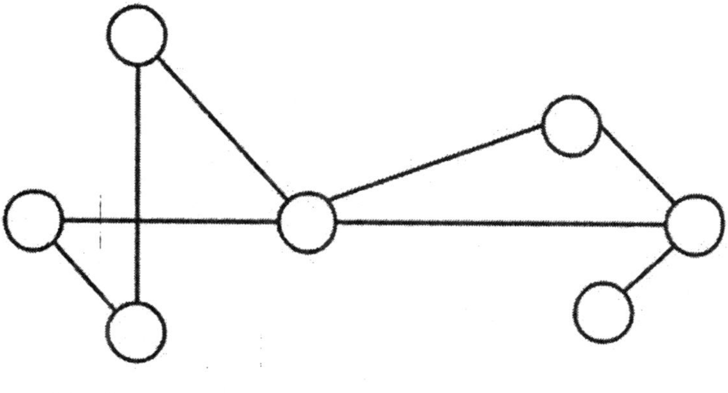

Mesh Network consists of a number of nodes linked together in such a way that sometimes data from one has to pass the third part to reach the destination.

Ring Network

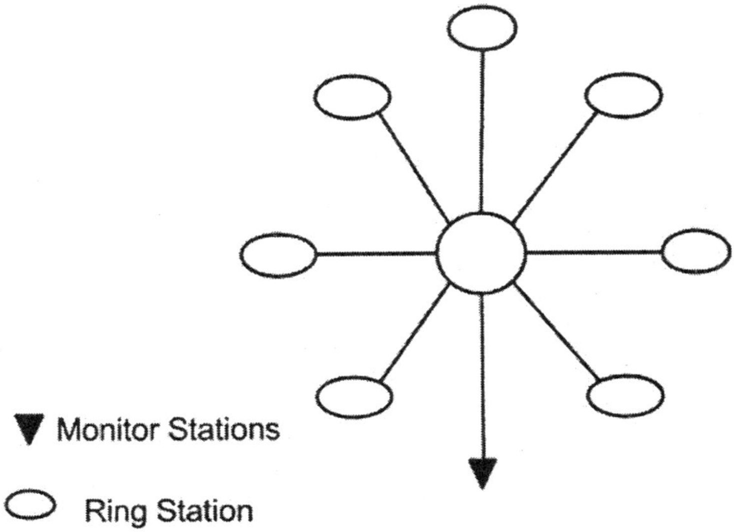

It consists of a number of nodes interconnected with each other in the form of a ring and transmission is in one direction. In such a system data is communicated very speedily.

Fully Connected Network

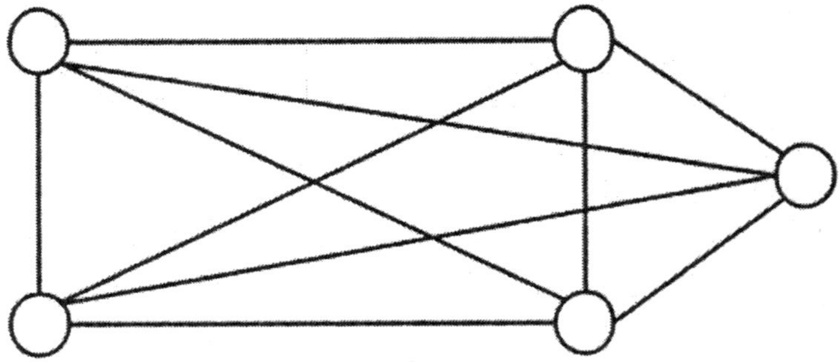

Fully connected Network consists of a number of nodes directly connected to each other

Multi-drop Network

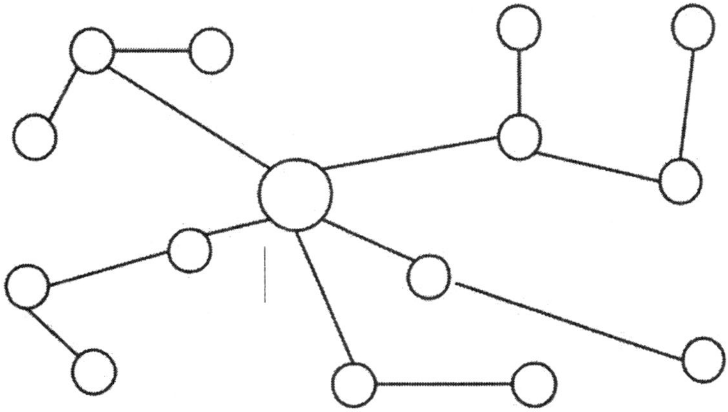

It has many terminals hanging off links to centre.

INTERNET

The Internet is a meta network, or net work of networks. It links up a global agglomeration of computer resources for public access. It began as an academic and research network, financially supported by the US government, but its phenomenal growth has brought in private and business uses in great number.

Internet is a system of linked computer networks, world wide in scope that facilitates data communication services such as remote login, file transfer, electronic mail and news groups. It is a way of connecting existing computer networks that greatly extends the reach of participating system. Internet is a meta network on to which millions of computers are hooked-up. This is a venue of information exchange. Millions of databases and files are available on the Internet . It is a conglomeration of smaller networks and other connected machines spanning the entire globe. According to the Internet Society, it consists today to cover 30,ooo networks in 96 countries. As on 31 March 2011, the estimated total number of Internet users was 2.095 billion(30.2% of world population) In 2013 the Internet users in developed countries constitute 77% while in developing countries 31%. It is estimated that in 1993 the Internet carried only 1% of the information flowing through two-way telecommunication, by 2000 this figure had grown to 51% and by 2007 more that 97% of all telecommunicated information was carried over the Internet. Around the world, each country has at least one backbone network that operates at very high speed and carries the bulk of the traffic.

Internet offers information on demand. No one filters or decides what information is most important or the most relevant for the user. The user is in charge of tapping the vast resources of the Internet. Several on-line services which include sending e-mails, searching information sources, chat with people lccated at far off places, involve in exchange of information among people with identical professional interest are available in the Internet. One can provide new publications in the net through millions of websites.

INTERNET SERVICES

Most traditional communications media including telephone, music ,film and televisions are being reshaped or redefined by th e Internet, giving birth to new services such as voice over internet protocol(VOIP) and Internet protocol television (IPTV). Newspaper, book and other print publishing are adapting to website technology, or are reshaped into blogging and web feeds. The Internet has enabled and accelerated new forms of human interactions through instant messaging, Internet forums and social networking. Online shopping has boomed both for major retail outlets and small artisans and traders. Business-to-business and financial services on the Internet affect supply chains across entire industries. Some of the important Internet services are given under.

i) Electronic Mail (e-mail)

Electronic mail is a most widely distributed form of electronic communication through computer networking. It is a mechanism for one-to-one correspondence, and sometimes one-to –few. It is much faster and message reaches the destination within seconds. The popular email services are:

Gmail

Gmail is possibly the best of the free mail service providers with simple user-friendly system for storing, sending and reading emails.

Yahoo mail

Yahoo mail is one of the best free email service providers on both the web and mobile services. Storage offered is unlimited and the service includes social networking , instant chat messaging , SMS texting etc

Outlook.com

It is Microsoft's replacement for the popular hot mail.com free email service. With the most up-to-date design, Outlool.com incorporates social network connections.

Zoho mail

The features of Zoho mail include calendar, task manager, notes and instant that and business applications, makes Zoho mail to be a great option for professionals

SOCIAL NETWORKING SERVICE

A social networking service is a platform to build social networks or social relations among people who share interests, activities, backgrounds or real-life connections. The Internet has enabled entirely new forms of social interaction. Many people use the WWW to access news, weather and sports reports, to plan and book vacations and to find out more about the interests. People use chat, messaging and email to make and stay in touch with friends worldwide sometimes in the same way as some previously had pen pals. Most social network services are web-based and provide means for users to interact over the internet. Popular services widely used worldwide are Facebook, Twitter, Orkut, Google+ , Tumblr etc.

SUBJECT GATEWAYS

The Subject Gateways are specialised catalogues in which the information has been selected and organised by a person or an organisation. It is also known as guide to information sources or a bibliographic guide, a literature guide to reference materials etc. It is a kind of meta-bibliography.

Google directory, Yahoo directory, WWW virtual library, The Internet public library, Infomine, Academic info. etc are some of the examples to subject gateways.

ELECTRONIC BUSINESS

E-Business involves business processes spanning the entire value chain. Electronic purchasing and supply chain: electronic purchasing management, processing orders electronically, handling customer service, and cooperating with business partners.

TELECOMMUTING

Remote work is facilitated by tools such as groupware, virtual networks, conference calling, video conferencing and voice over IP (VOIP)

CROUDSOURCING OR OUTSOURCING

Internet provides a particularly good venue for croudsourcing (outsourcing) tasks to distributed group of people since individuals tend to be more open to web-based projects where they are not being physically judged or scrutinised and thus can feel more comfortable sharing.

INTRANET

Intranet is an internal network of an organisation, using the TCP/IP . To provide an intranet, an organisation must have its on LAN or WAN, a web server and browsing software for users.

EXTRANET

Extranet is private network using the Internet protocol to share a company's information with suppliers, partners, customers or the other businesses. An extranet can be viewed as an Intranet opened to a wider range of users so as to provide a company with an effective forum for work on projects, obtaining bids, sharing of news, joint training programmes and ongoing communication over cooperation. Security is crucial so that firewalls, Encryption and other network and computer security features are essential.

Bibliography

Anil K Dhiman. Basiscs of information technology for libraries and information. New Delhi, ESS ESS, 2003

Devarajan, G. Information Technology in Libraries, New Delhi, ESS ESS, 1999.

Devarajan, G and Rahelamma, AV, Ed. Library computerization in India, New Delhi, ESS ESS, 1990.

Devarajan, G , Ed. Progress in information technology. New Delhi, ESS ESS, 1996.

Feather, John and Sturges, Paul. International encyclopedia of information and library science.London, Routledge,1997.

Freeman, Alan. Computer Desktop Encyclopedia. New York: McGraw-Hill, 2001

Gates, Bill. The Road Ahead. Rev. ed. London: Penguin Books, 1996

Gilster, Ron. PC hardware: a beginner's guide. New York: McGraw-Hill, 2001

hanna, JK. Information technology in the libraries. New Delhi, Pragathy, 1994.

Pandey, VC, Ed. Networking: The foundations for information society.

Ravichandra Rao, IK. Library automation. New Delhi, New Age, 1996.

Ravindran Asari, K. Informatics: An Introduction. New Delhi: Ane Books, 2010

Sharma, Pandey S.K. Fundamentals of library automation

Tedd, LA.An introduction to computer-based library systems. London, Hydon,1977.

Turban, Efraim, et al. Introduction to Information Technology. New York: John Wiley & Sons, 2000

Williams, Brian K. et al. Using Information Technology: A practical introduction to computer and communications. 2nd ed. Boston: Irwin McGraw-Hill, 1999.

INDEX